Journal of Prisoners
on Prisons

I0118209

... allowing our experiences and analysis to be added to the forum that will constitute public opinion could help halt the disastrous trend toward building more fortresses of fear which will become in the 21ˢᵗ century this generation's monuments to failure.

Jo-Ann Mayhew (1988)

Volume 22
Number 2
2013

JOURNAL OF PRISONERS ON PRISONS

EDITORIAL STAFF:

Editor-in-Chief:	Bob Gaucher	Issue Editors:	Susan Nagelsen
Associate Editors:	Susan Nagelsen		Charles Huckelbury
	Charles Huckelbury	Prisoners' Struggles Editor:	Kevin Walby
Managing Editors:	Justin Piché	Book Review Editor:	Pat Derby
	Mike Larsen	Editorial Assistants:	Ashley Chen
			Sarah Fiander

EDITORIAL BOARD:

Stacie Alarie	Giselle Dias	Tara Lyons	Rose Ricciardelli
Bree Carlton	Danial Dos Santos	MaDonna Maidment	Jeffrey Ian Ross
Mielle Chandler	Aaron Doyle	Katharina Maier	Viviane Saleh-Hanna
Vicki Chartrand	Maritza Felices-Luna	Joane Martel	Judah Schept
Bell Gale Chevigny	Sylvie Frigon	Shadd Maruna	Renita Seabrook
Panagiota Chrisovergis	Christine Gervais	Erin McCuaig	Rashad Shabazz
Elizabeth Comack	Anne-Marie Grondin	Dawn Moore	Lisa Smith
Howard Davidson	Kelly Hannah-Moffatt	Melissa Munn	Dale Spencer
Claire Delisle	Stacey Hannem	Mecke Nagel	Brian Chad Starks
Leah DeVellis	Jennifer Kilty	Karen Raddon	Kelly Struthers Montford
Eugene Dey	Michael Lenza	Stephen C. Richards	Matt Yeager

The *Journal of Prisoners on Prisons* publishes two volumes a year. Its purpose is to encourage research on a wide range of issues related to crime, justice, and punishment by prisoners and former prisoners. Donations to the *JPP* are welcomed.

SUBMISSIONS:

Prisoners and former prisoners are encouraged to submit original papers, collaborative essays, discussions transcribed from tape, book reviews, and photo or graphic essays that have not been published elsewhere. The *Journal* does not usually publish fiction or poetry. The *Journal* will publish articles in either French or English. Articles should be no longer than 20 pages typed and double-spaced or legibly handwritten. Electronic submissions are gratefully received. Writers may elect to write anonymously or under a pseudonym. For references cited in an article, the writer should attempt to provide the necessary bibliographic information. Refer to the references cited in this issue for examples. Submissions are reviewed by members of the Editorial Board. Selected articles are corrected for composition and returned to the authors for their approval before publication. Papers not selected are returned with editor's comments. Revised papers may be resubmitted. Please submit bibliographical and contact information, to be published alongside articles unless otherwise indicated.

SUBCRIPTIONS, SUBMISSIONS AND ALL OTHER CORRESPONDENCE:

Journal of Prisoners on Prisons
c/o Justin Piché, Assistant Professor
Department of Criminology, University of Ottawa   e-mail: jpp@uottawa.ca
Ottawa, Ontario, Canada K1N 6N5   website: www.jpp.org

SUBCRIPTION RATES FOR 2013:	One Year	Two Years	Three Years
Prisoners	$15.00	$28.00	$40.00
Individuals	$30.00	$56.00	$80.00
Prison Libraries & Schools, Libraries & Institutions	$60.00	$110.00	$150.00

Subscriptions by mail are payable in Canadian or American dollars. In Canada, 5% HST must be added to all orders. We encourage subscriptions made online at http://www.press.uottawa.ca/JPP_subscription

INDIVIDUAL COPIES AND BACK ISSUES:

Each regular issue is $15 and each double-issue is $25 (Canadian dollars) + shipping costs. In Canada, 5% HST must be added to all orders. Back issues can be purchased from the University of Ottawa Press at www.press.uottawa.ca/subject/criminology. If interested in obtaining issues that are out of print, please contact the *JPP* directly. Further information regarding course orders and distribution can be obtained from the University of Toronto Press at:

University of Toronto Press Inc.	phone:	1-800-565-9523
5201 Dufferin Street	fax:	1-800-221-9985
Toronto, Ontario, Canada M3H 5T8	e-mail:	utpbooks@utpress.utoronto.ca
	website:	www.utpress.utoronto.ca/utp_D1/home.htm

Co-published by the University of Ottawa Press and the *Journal of Prisoners on Prisons*.

Printed and Bound in Canada

ISSN 0838-164X
ISBN 978-0-7766-0943-0

In This Issue

EDITORS' INTRODUCTION

Divergent Voices: Discourses and Perspective
Susan Nagelsen and Charles Huckelbury

Western prisons have been, and continue to be, described in various terms and using a broad range of images, each description relying on the interpretation of the individual, whether prisoner, guard, visitor, academic, or other interested party. It will come as no surprise, then, that the various descriptions, many self-serving, often conflict and even contradict each other. M. C. Escher's famous lithograph, *Ascending and Descending*, serves as a metaphor for this inconsistency, with some of the figures going up the staircase as others descend, all of them retracing the same path in perpetual lockstep.

When applied to Western prisons, this dual nature frequently finds its expression in the public face of the administrators and staff (safety and security) versus the private face (neglect and brutality). This issue of the *Journal of Prisoners on Prisons* (JPP) therefore offers an examination of the prison experience, given voice by those who have endured it, framed in terms Escher would doubtless understand and appreciate.

Colin Scholl opens the discussion with a personal narrative of what an American prison is like, in response to frequently asked questions by those on the outside. Scholl's stark recitation reveals its brutal nature. He shows us the life that many prisoners have known and to which they can relate. For at least twenty years, his life is totally controlled, from the time he gets up until the time he goes to bed, and he brings the reader into his struggle against the regimented routine and the constant refrain that he is worthless.

An Australian prisoner, Craig Minogue, recounts his adventure in the absurd world of prison by detailing the bureaucratic obstacles encountered when attempting to get clear plastic covers for his books, which on the face of it is a reasonable request. The incoherent staff responses and the bureaucratic bungling make this simple request resemble a private in the military requesting nuclear launch codes from his commander in chief. The surreal aspect of the account is that Craig Minogue encountered the prison administration's ire after he successfully mounted a campaign to reduce drug abuse by prisoners. His narrative thus parallels Escher's creations perhaps more faithfully than many outsiders would believe, but his is no optical illusion.

1

Eugene Dey follows with a poignant description of the decline and death of a California prisoner trapped in a system in which sending a prisoner out in a body bag elicits no more reaction than swatting a fly. Diagnosed with hepatitis C long after his symptoms appeared, the lack of medical care produced a terminal condition that could have been controlled in its earlier stages. Freddy was an inveterate armed robber who made no excuses for his choices, but as Eugene Dey points out, even such a man merits fundamental medical treatment and concern for his physical health.

In perhaps a classic example of the bizarre and self-defeating nature of American prisons, Jon Marc Taylor delves into the labyrinthine (and lucrative) nature of prison phone services. Given the obscene profits phone companies reap from overcharging prisoners and their families for a few minutes of conversation, Jon Marc Taylor devised a plan to channel some or all of the prison's percentage of the profits into a fund for higher education. He recruited a variety of supporters, including state legislators who agreed to sponsor such a bill. Everything looked on track until the actual amount of money moderated the enthusiasm. Rather than the ten million dollars originally estimated, the actual amount was six times that figure, a sum the Department of Corrections and the Missouri legislature categorically refused to allocate for higher education. As in most things American, it was about the money.

Confirming the punitive nature of prison comes Timothy Muise's powerful and disheartening essay on the persistent reluctance – and often refusal – to grant U.S. prisoners any kind of release prior to parole or the completion of their sentences. Ignoring both statistical evidence and historical precedent, states continue to prefer long-term incarceration to compassionate release, even for infirm and geriatric prisoners. Fiscal constraints, traditionally a strong motivator, fail to sufficiently move those charged with making the decisions to consider authorizing the release of terminally ill prisoners with literally weeks to live. As Muise reveals, the drive to punish until death remains the dominant philosophy.

Grace Gámez then takes us on a *tour de force* through the chronological events that have enabled a patriarchal society to treat current and former prisoners as if they were zombies, that is, neither alive nor dead and having no intrinsic worth. Her mastery of historical precedent and command of information bring to these pages a powerful argument for reversing the retribution juggernaut and acknowledging the fundamental humanity of every citizen.

But, as Grant Tietjen corroborates, the federal prison system in the United States is as equally pernicious as the state's scheme when it comes to both the treatment of its prisoners and in preparing them for re-entry to society. His detailed account of his foray into the system and his subsequent attempts to acclimate a prison mentality to the real world beyond the walls is part of a comprehensive analysis of the often-surreal nature of living life exclusively at the mercy of others. Tietjen's experiences have produced a compelling story about his efforts to mentor and comfort others who have traveled the same path.

Given the sheer numbers of men and women incarcerated in the United States, encountering innocent people consigned to cages no longer surprises. It should, however, continue to alarm. Mwandishi Mitchell points out that wrongful convictions create victims no less than the actual offenses themselves, many of who find it impossible to leave the trauma behind once they are released. To their credit, some states are moving to enact greater safeguards, including mandatory DNA testing, to prevent innocent men and women from going to prison. However, as Mwandishi Mitchell points out, the road remains long and strewn with both philosophical and legislative obstacles.

And yet, all the Escherian implications notwithstanding, there is light in even the deepest recesses of the system. Colin McGregor, serving time in a Canadian prison, describes what can happen when prisoners take control of their own futures, at least to the extent they can. McGregor's paper addresses literacy efforts inside a particular prison and the determination of an older prisoner to learn to read. Getting help from a non-profit, Colin McGregor became a certified tutor and was able to watch while that older prisoner mastered the task he had chosen for himself. Although the non-profit lost its funding, Colin McGregor remains optimistic about grassroots efforts to continue reading programs on the inside.

Throughout its twenty-five-year history, the *JPP* has provided a consistent forum for those whose voices would have otherwise remained mute. Part of that mission has been a vigorous opposition to censorship, a frequently used weapon against prisoners' attempts to resist their conditions of imprisonment and always an effort to convince the authors that they have nothing worthwhile to add to public discourse. That is not to say that we have agreed with every position appearing in the journal. As one researcher put it, "there are as many prisons as there are prisoners" (Sykes, 1958, p. 63). Our focus has been and continues to be on getting those voices, irrespective of our reaction to them, into the public arena as long as the peer-reviewed submissions fall within clearly defined editorial parameters. We continue that tradition by closing this section of prisoner narratives with a paper by Miguel Zaldivar.

Miguel Zaldivar, a federal prisoner in the United States, agrees with the other writers in this issue that prison is distinctly an unpleasant place. However, whereas those contributors criticize the operational ethos, structured oppression, and systematic brutality of the prison itself, Miguel Zaldivar places much of the blame for the inhumane prison environment squarely on the men and women behind the walls. In his view, every complaint by a prisoner about prison conditions fails to acknowledge the prisoners' complicity in erecting and sustaining the physical and psychological dungeons that hold them. Indeed, he assigns them primary responsibility for their Stygian existence for the same reason Mallory wanted to scale Everest: because they are there.

Such a proposition is in our view ironically refuted by Miguel Zaldivar's description of some of his own encounters with prison officials. While his standpoint differs significantly from those of the majority of *JPP* contributors, his position is one that is shared by many prisoners and thus merits exposition and the debate that will follow.

REFERENCES

Sykes, Gresham M. (1958) *The Society of Captives: A Study of a Maximum Security Prison*, Princeton (NJ): Princeton University Press.

ABOUT THE ISSUE EDITORS

Susan Nagelsen is an Associate Editor of the *Journal of Prisoners on Prisons* and the Director of the Writing Program at New England College in Henniker, New Hampshire. Her book, *Exiled Voices: Portals of Discovery*, is a collection of writings by women and men in prisons across the country. Her most recent published work appears in the *New Plains Review*, *IdeaGems* and *Ephipanymag*.org.

Charles Huckelbury is an Associate Editor of the *JPP*. He has received four PEN awards for fiction and nonfiction and is the author of two books of poetry. He also writes a monthly newsletter for the Prisons Foundation in Washington, D.C.

What is Prison Like?
Colin Scholl

A few times people have asked me what prison is like. I have never known how to answer that. It is such a huge question. It is a whole different world. It would take reams of paper to tell someone what prison is like, because it is like nothing people on the outside have ever known.

Some people on the outside have queer ideas of prison. They think it is something akin to a vacation. Let me assure you, it is nothing like a vacation.

Since I cannot really tell you what prison is like in terms that you would really understand, I will not try. I can, however, tell you what a twenty-year prison sentence means to me.

A twenty-year prison sentence means a million things to me, because as twenty years in prison suggests, it is the major part of my adult life.

It means enduring my reduction to a third-class citizen in the eyes of most people. It means decades of discrimination from the courts and public. "Inmate", "prisoner", "convict" – each has a unique, and strictly pejorative, use in the media and pop culture. Those terms slowly work themselves into my psyche and become the defining characteristic of my being, changing me in a way that hurts my soul.

It means the court will turn a blind eye to any act against me unless it causes "demonstrable and permanent injury", so when I am stripped naked and left in a concrete box with nothing but a toilet for four days without cause, as a prisoner, I have no recourse in the courts. When I am beaten to a bloody mess while in handcuffs, as a prisoner, I am more likely to encounter a jury that will conclude that I deserved what I got, regardless of the circumstances.

It means that if I am killed by another prisoner, my murderer will have twenty-four months added to his sentence, the same amount of time you would receive for killing your neighbour's dog.

It means that after being spared a life sentence, anything that happens to me is well deserved, because I am getting out.

It means two decades of censorship where I am told what books or magazines I can read, what photos I can look at, what things I can write, what films I can watch, what clothes I can wear, even the way I can cut my hair, and where every letter coming in and going out is read and inspected.

It means a complete lack of privacy and a complete lack of concern for my well being for twenty years.

It means a cold indifference to my suffering, my physical, emotional and mental health.

It means three meals a day of the poorest quality food that the least amount of money can buy without killing the prison's population.

It means that I am constantly told, in a thousand ways, that I cannot be rehabilitated, that I am not worth the resources to even try to help, that I am morally and mentally inferior, and to try and help someone like me is foolish.

It means being told for twenty years that I will never amount to anything.

It means convincing myself daily that my life has value, even when the rest of the world tells me that I am worthless.

It means twenty years of wondering what my potential is and yearning to find out.

It means being subjected to incomprehensible punishments deemed "necessary to maintain institutional security", such as being sprayed with burning chemicals that blister my skin and make patches of my hair fall out.

It means being placed in cages for hours that are just big enough to stand in.

It means being zip-tied and made to lay face down in the dirt, mud, and snow, stripped naked every day and inspected with a flash light, placed on "potty watch" with an adult diaper duck-taped to my waist and legs, without a shred of clothing, barefoot, and belly-chained, forced to fill a diaper with excrement three times before they will consider my release.

It means I cannot hold a woman or experience a gentle loving touch for two decades.

It means being incapable of taking care of my grandparents and parents as they reach their final years.

It means not being able to have children or a family.

A twenty-year sentence means constant contemplation of a wasted life, a continued despair as to my inability to accomplish anything significant with my remaining years. A life spent watching as each of my family members and friends die or slowly drift away, leaving me in a vacuum, devoid of any enduring relationships.

It is a persistent dashing of my hopes.

It is a permanent experiment in self-delusion, as I struggle to convince myself that there is still hope.

It is a compounding of second upon second, minute upon minute, hour upon hour of wasted existence, and decade upon decade of mental and emotional torture.

These are futile attempts to describe the indescribable. It is like trying to describe a broken heart or communicate what it is like to mourn the death of your soul mate. The words to convey the pain do not exist. It is as if I am experiencing the broken heart of knowing I will never love, or be loved in any normal sense of the word, while mourning the death of the man I could have, and should have been. The only difference is that I can never recover, because the pain is renewed each morning when I wake up to realize I am still here. It is always a fresh day of despair, lived over and over for twenty years.

So as you can see, this is not like a vacation.

Putting it to paper I can see more clearly that, although you may understand the words, you cannot understand the experience and how it affects my soul. And that is a good thing.

ABOUT THE AUTHOR

Colin Scholl is a prisoner at California State Prison, Los Angeles County. He is currently pursuing an M.A. in Sociology.

Chicken Soup
Craig W. J. Minogue

I have been in prison since 1986, and at first I raged against the system with violence, barricades, and fires, but through a slow process I have matured into a jailhouse lawyer and academic. I have also come to accept the appropriateness of my being separated from the community because of my actions. That is not to say I am happy about it or do not resist when resistance is called for. In 2008, I was transferred to the Marngoneet Correctional Centre after twenty-two years in maximum-security prisons. Marngoneet is a programs prison. Paraphrasing their promotional material, the prison provides:

> An intensive level of treatment and offender management activity to prepare for a successful crime-free release from prison. There are 3 x 100 bed neighbourhoods (one protection and two mainstream) which function as therapeutic communities where all prisoners participate as members of the neighbourhood community.

> Accommodation in each bed neighbourhood comprises: one 40-cell unit, each cell with shower and toilet. The 60 other beds are in self-catering accommodation with: 2 lock-up accommodations of 6 cells which each have a shower and toilet; 6 flat-style accommodations with six bedrooms each and 2 shared bathroom facilities; 3 cottage style accommodations with four bedrooms and 2 shared bathroom facilities. All have a lounge area and kitchenette. The carpeted bedrooms have a bed, a desk, and a wardrobe the like of which could be found at an Ikea store.

> Each neighbourhood has a targeted clinical purpose: protection and sex offender; violent offender and drug/alcohol offender. Prisoners cook, clean and manage budget and their own hygiene in the 4- and 6-bed units (independent living/self-catering) and take responsibility for themselves and each other, working together with custodial, clinical and vocational staff to achieve a safe, secure and therapeutic neighbourhood.

In the self-catering accommodation, the prison allocates forty-eight dollars per week per person to spend on a set list of food. There is an electric stove, microwave oven, electrical appliances, fridge and all types of cooking utensils and equipment. It seems to work well for those men who do not want to buy junk. They deliver the food twice a week. How this system works depends on who the men are and what they want to buy. Older more organized men have a good stock of food on hand, but some of the men live from hand to mouth with milk, bread and ice cream. I am in a four-bed accommodation in physical and social conditions that I have to say are very good.

Despite accepting the appropriateness of my being here and the very good physical living conditions, I am still held coercively with the threat of violence. At this Therapeutic Treatment Community there are omnipresent levels of surveillance, categorisation, and classification, which ensure the assessments, management, and treatment interventions through programs and policies designed to reduce re-offending are relentlessly applied. There is a Custodial Assessment, a Clinical Assessment, a Treatment Management Plan, Pre- and Post-Psychometric Testing regimes, a Vocational Services Assessment and an Accommodation Plan, which combine to constitute a Whole of Services Assessment that is overseen by a Review and Assessment Committee. There are Individual Management Plan Files, a Clinical File, a Psychometric Assessment Register, a Clinical Services Register, Service Reports and many other reports, case notes, case review entries, and file notes. Michel Foucault says that in "the harshest of prisons" the disciplinary discourse holds over the prisoner the inescapable reality that the custodial officer and the psychologist will "note the slightest irregularity in your conduct" (Foucault, 1991, p. 299). And so it is at Marngoneet Correctional Centre (see Minogue, 2011).

There is a no-man's-land barrier, surveillance, a wall topped with razor wire. To drive home the coercive and threatening nature of it all, every other week hundreds of gunshots echo loudly around the walls here as prison staff practice their aim with nine millimetre, large-capacity magazine weapons at the pistol range that is right next to the prison. And there are many more, less obvious ways in which my life here is a moment-to-moment battle, which would not be obvious to the casual visitor. My life here is experienced as continual conflict, but in comfortable conditions. The story about the clear Contact to cover books and the chicken phenomenon will illustrate what I mean.

In July 2011, I received a three-volume set of academic books about social research methodology and I wanted to cover them with clear Contact to keep them in good condition. I did not have enough for the job remaining on a large roll of Contact I had bought a few years previous, so on July 29, I asked prison staff for a Special Spend Form. I filled out my part of the form requesting the clear Contact for covering the books, and a prison officer filled out his part. From there, I had my request approved by a more senior officer. I knew this was going to be a contentious issue here, as security and control are more intense now than ever before, so I wrote a cover letter to the people who buy these types of items and said:

> I have ordered a roll of clear contact to cover some books. I bought clear contact at this location in June 2008. I have in fact, bought and used contact to cover books at every prison I have been in for the past 25 years. Occasionally however, some staff think that it is a forbidden item. It is not. If there is a problem with my buying this item then I ask that I be advised who has made the decision and on what grounds, as it would be my intention to advocate that it would be appropriate for me to have access to this item, and I need to know with whom to advocate and on what terms. Thank you for your consideration.

The form was returned to me with a handwritten note saying "Cancelled, not permitted". So I asked, "Who says it is not permitted?" I received a second copy of the form with a note saying, "Craig, as per Collators, this item is not permitted. Thanks". Many emails were exchanged, and I was mistakenly given copies of them attached to the form with the handwritten note (the Collator is the Security and Intelligence Officer of the prison).

So in August I wrote to the local Manager in the area in which I am housed and said:

> I have bought clear Contact on special spends to cover books in Pentridge Prison's H Division 25 years ago and I still have some of the books I covered in H Division with me now. I have used Contact to cover books in the Acacia High Security Unit at Barwon. Contact which was bought on the special spend at Barwon. I have had books covered in Contact for over 25 years in prison. I have even bought a roll of Contact here at prison 2 years ago. Contact to cover books is clear, the piece attached over this text demonstrates [the illustration imperative at work]. The prison system has x-ray machines, drug-sniffing dogs and highly trained staff [seriously they do]. I therefore, see no real need to restrict clear Contact

at this medium security prison. I have had 3 academic books sent to me. They cost $162.00 and are books I will keep and use for the rest of my life. I would like to cover them with Contact to protect them. I ask that the decision by the Collator to refuse me access to the common office, library and home stationary item to be reconsidered.

The local manager said I could buy the Contact, so I asked for another form and filled out my part, and a prison officer filled out his part. From there, I had it approved by a more senior officer and lodged the form. The form was again returned to me, this time with an even larger handwritten note saying, "Craig, I have checked with Security Manager and this item is prohibited – Cancelled". So I met with the staff who do the Special Spends, and I asked what the problem is. They told me that the Security Manager said, "He could use Contact to hide things under it".

I said, "It's clear, what could I hide?"
The answer: "Invisible things!"
But I said, "If they are invisible, why would I need to hide them?"
The answer: "We don't know, that's just what the Security Manager says".

So I complained to the local Manager and he said he would take the issue to the Leadership Team. I wrote a short cover letter to be attached to all the documents in the matter and said:

There seems to be an imperative that if possible, items should be made of clear material to allow inspection, like pens, highlighters, and now even some electrical items. Contact is clear, like the piece which covers the text you are now reading. [This was the last piece I had, not big enough for a book, but big enough to make the point].

The local Manager then told me that the matter was being considered by the Leadership Team. By September 2011, I had not received a response from the Leadership Team, so I wrote to the general Manager of the prison and asked to be advised of the outcome. I did not receive a response. In October, I had a meeting with the General Manager to get her approval to send out some art, so I asked what was happening with the Contact issue. She said, "Oh yes, you can have that".

I said, "Thanks for that, but I need that advice in writing from you or the Special Spends people will not buy it for me". The General Manager said she would send me a written approval.

A week later I had heard nothing, so when I saw the Executive Officer of the prison in passing, the General Manager's secretary, and I took the opportunity to ask what was going on with the Contact issue. She told me that the Leadership Team could not settle the matter, so it went to the Director of Prisons for a decision, and he decided that I could have the clear Contact for covering books. The Executive Officer said if I had a new Special Spends Form delivered to her, she would make sure it was processed. I asked for another form. I filled out my part of the form, and a prison officer filled out his part. Once I had it approved by a more senior officer, I asked that it be delivered directly to the Executive Officer. The prison officer said that he would do that.

A week later, I saw the Executive Officer in passing and asked how it went, but she told me she had not received the form. So I confronted the officer who said he delivered the form and told him that I had just spoken to the Executive Officer who said the form was not delivered to her. The officer then changed his story and said he put it in the General Manager's mailbox at the front gate. I told the officer I did not believe him and insisted that he call the Executive Officer and sort it out. He called while I stood there and listened to his very unconvincing lies. The Executive Officer said I should fill out another form, which I did, and she personally came and collected it a short time later. A few days later, she told me that she had attached the email from the director of prisons saying I could buy the clear Contact and she had delivered it personally to the Special Spends staff with an instruction that they must buy the item.

On November 17 I received the clear Contact—Merry Christmas to me! But why did the Security Manager have such a bee in his bonnet about this? To answer that question we need to go back to September 2010, when there was a major problem at this prison with the drug called buprenorphine (called Bupe by prisoners). At the time, the everyday conversation was about Bupe, and as Bupe sounded like 'soup', it was referred to as 'Chicken Soup', or 'Chicken' for short. A lexicon developed. 'Chicken hawks', the men who were chasing the 'Chicken', were seen to swoop in and out of 'Chicken coops' (the cells and accommodation areas where it was happening). Chicken hawks from other parts of the prison would stand at the entrance to other areas 'scratching around' for some Chicken. And scratching is an appropriate description, as the men using this drug would develop skin irritations and have a nervous aspect and even paw at the ground with their feet like a chicken scratching for seed. "Have you got Chicken?", "Do you want Chicken?", and "The Chicken hawks are scratching around" became a running joke.

I had an idea to change the Chicken discourse. I designed a *No Chicken Here* art initiative, which did *much more* to cause prisoners to question the Chicken phenomenon than all their drug tests, disciplinary actions and searches could have ever achieved. In twenty-four hours, my *No Chicken Here* campaign completely changed the discourse in a profound way. The prison was powerless against the Chicken epidemic, but I changed the running joke to: "No Chicken here, man". People would pass each other on the path and say as a greeting, "No Chicken here, man".

People were empowered by the graffiti-like public art initiative to identify themselves with opposing the minority, but generally disruptive, Chicken culture. I fixed the *No Chicken Here* signs with clear contact to many surfaces around the prison. I put them on light poles and signs, on electrical switch boxes and even on the doors of staff areas, all in a kind of Banksy-like guerilla-art campaign. My actions caused great controversy with the staff and it was an agenda item on the Leadership Team's meeting for that week.

I was told the security Manager was filthy on the *No Chicken Here* campaign and wanted to kick my head: "Who does this Minogue think he is?" The other members of the Leadership Team understood it on some level and decided that no action should be taken against me. So when it came time some months later for me to request the clear Contact, it is my guess that the *No Chicken Here* campaign was still stuck in the security Manager's craw, and it was this that was in fact behind the resistance I faced, and which I overcame.

So, it remains a battle after twenty-six years, a battle punctuated by a few hundred gunshots every other week just to remind me what would happen if I got it into my head to decline the hospitality and comfortable conditions that the casual visitor would see me enjoying.

REFERENCES

Foucault, Michel (1991) *Discipline and Punish: The Birth of the Prison* (Allan Sheridan, trans.), London: Penguin Books.

Minogue, Craig (2011) "Is the Foucauldian Conception of Disciplinary Power Still at Work in Contemporary Forms of Imprisonment?", *Foucault Studies*, 11: 178-192.

ABOUT THE AUTHOR

Dr. Craig W. J. Minogue has survived prison since 1986. Completing a BA (Hons) in 2005, he was awarded a research-based PhD in Applied Ethics in 2012. He can be contacted by email at craig2016@bigpond.com or by mail at the address below:

PO Box 273
Corio, Victoria,
Australia 3214

www.craigminogue.org

A Requiem for Freddy
Eugene Dey

His liver destroyed by hepatitis C, Robert Hagenson did not receive a transplant but a type of early parole – in a body bag. His sudden deterioration and death hit many of his fellow prisoners hard, particularly me. Watching a man die by inches is unsettling, especially when he is a fellow prisoner and a friend.

Everyone called him "Freddy". I forgot why. He was forty-five years old when he began serving a sentence of twenty-five years to life for an armed robbery committed in 1997. Barely over five feet tall, his body covered in tattoos and his head shaved clean, he looked every bit the convict and criminal.

Freddy walked ramrod straight. With half of a cigar clamped between his teeth, he always had a determined look in his eye, even if only on his way to the water fountain. He reminded me of a soldier on patrol. A blunt-spoken grouch, Freddy vociferously said what he thought. Notorious for his rants against God, government, and the GOP, Freddy rarely let the facts get in the way of his opinions.

"George Bush needs a few good men!" Freddy loved to scream out. As the 2004 presidential election converged with the debate surrounding the war in Iraq, he was quick to challenge anyone on politics. Freddy hated Bush, but he did not discriminate either. "You pigs got it too easy", Freddy would yell, mainly to antagonize the guards. "It's time to get a real job". His legendary sarcasm complimented his belligerent tirades. No one, including Freddy, really took it seriously.

As cellmates, Freddy and I became friends in 2004. Anyone willing to put up with me bouncing off the walls at all hours, coupled with incessant racket from my typewriter, earns my undying friendship and respect. We remained friends even after I moved to another cell.

Freddy's criminal career spanned four decades and numerous prison terms. In the mould of the hardened criminal, Freddy was a robber – a stick-up man from the old school and he harboured no illusions. On many occasions, he told me he expected to die in prison, but he never expressed a desire to die from the hepatitis C virus (HCV).

"These cry-babies think they're getting out", Freddy would tell me. "This is the end of the line, buddy. Get your head out of your ass and do your time". It was true. We all suffered from the glimmer-of-hope syndrome. We convince ourselves hope is just on the horizon, but Freddy was right. When lifers like us start talking about the streets, we sound like fools. Freddy pulled no punches. "I'm never getting out", he'd say casually. This sober dose of reality hit me hard for many years to come: "I'm a criminal and I'll die in prison".

Freddy's first real attempt to seek medical attention began in the summer of 2004. He had lost a lot of weight. Once muscular, Freddy was now thin as a rail. "I don't feel right", Freddy told me one morning, "Something is wrong with me. I keep forgetting stuff, and I can't sleep". I know nothing of medicine. Weight loss and insomnia are symptoms of liver disease. Loss of memory is a sign of liver failure. Naively, I thought him too ornery to fall prey to illness. I helped him anyway, because that is what we do.

In the next few months, Freddy saw a half dozen different prison doctors. Rather than see a specialist, or even just one doctor who possesses an intimate knowledge about a patient's condition, prisoners will often go months without seeing the same doctor twice. "Every doctor has a different opinion, and they all tell you something different", Freddy complained to me one day. I can still see the lines of old age on a wrinkled face accelerated by a deadly virus. Since he always complained, I saw no real reason to worry.

August 2004 blood tests, however, showed Freddy's liver enzymes at double and triple the high range. These levels alarmed me. In obvious need of treatment, he received nothing but the run-around. By October, a slew of "unreadable", "partial", and "lost" test results, in addition to empty stares from the medical practitioners, greeted Freddy at every turn. In response to Freddy's pointed questions, they ordered more blood tests. I helped an angry Freddy file an administrative appeal.

A month later, the chief medical officer of the California Correctional Center cancelled Freddy's appeal. The CMO stated Hagenson waived his appeal rights by refusing to cooperate because he had grown angry with the medical staff. The appeal, ironically, had nothing to do with his attempt to seek treatment, but the complete breakdown in accountability. I did not know it at the time, but the entire medical department was broken. All I knew when I wrote the appeal was that Freddy still had not received treatment.

Prison is a breeding ground for all manner of blood-borne illnesses, especially pathogens like HCV. Tainted needles follow the path of the contraband drugs like the angel of death. Since Freddy had shared needles his whole life, he assumed he had HCV. I convinced him to keep going to medical. "Those motherfuckers are like vampires", Freddy complained, "All they do is take blood".

"I know, bro", I agreed, "Just quit busting their balls".

Freddy laughed. "I called them veterinarians".

I heard from numerous prisoners about his tirades at medical. The California Department of Corrections and Rehabilitation (CDCR) had medical technical assistants who were also guards – some were decent, but many made fatal decisions when they decided a prisoner needed rough treatment.

A liver biopsy in January 2005 not only confirmed HCV, but also disclosed that it had progressed to severe cirrhosis of the liver. Time was of the essence. A doctor told him he would soon be starting a regimen of interferon-ribavirin, known as combination drug therapy. Freddy had chronic HCV, considered an incurable disease. The combination drug therapy, however, has cleared the virus from many and greatly extended the lives of many others. For some, who have a certain strain, it does not work. But wonder drugs cannot even try to work their magic if they are not administered.

Months crept by. Chronic HCV is the end stage of life. Such a crucial juncture requires action, not indifference. More blood tests were taken, but still no treatment for Freddy. Then came July. Nearly a year from his first report of symptoms, prison doctors determined Freddy's ammonia levels were too high to qualify for treatment. Instead, they told him, his paperwork had been sent to the CDCR headquarters in Sacramento.

"They gave me a year or two to live", Freddy told me one day. I did not know what to say. Rarely at a loss for words, I silently walked the track with him. He seemed calm.

Freddy's tattoos caught my attention. The peacock on his forearm blended into a mosaic of mediocre body art, covering his dying body. They seemed to tell a sad story of a hard life. "Are you alright?", I asked. It seemed like a lame question. By now, he should have already been on the medication. This scenario played out too many times. Sending his paperwork to CDCR headquarters made no sense (deliberate...). Another round of delays, and the only therapy Freddy received was another layer of bureaucracy (indifference). Another year elapsed while his condition was treated like a procurement order.

At some point, excuses do not cut it. When they should say, "Sorry, our total incompetence as practitioners of medicine has allowed your narrow window of opportunity to close", instead they say, "Oh by the way, you are going to die". I am not going to lie. Many people, including the guards, consider telling the truth snitching. Some truths, however, need to be told.

Freddy loved to get high. He shot heroin his entire life. Like many in prison, he was a hardcore drug addict. Freddy committed robberies and shot dope. Nevertheless, he did not want to die. While he went through the process of trying to secure treatment, he promised himself he would not do drugs. For the most part, he stayed sober. He wanted to live.

"You can't live forever", he calmly said as we slowly walked around the track. "Now I can get the hell out of this place. I hate prison".

I believe his attempt at sobriety came to an abrupt end. As far as the truth is concerned, that is the best I can do. By October, massive gastrointestinal bleeding brought Freddy to death's door. One morning he vomited blood – and a lot of it, the first stage of liver failure. Organ failure is an excruciating death. I will never forget the look on his face, a look I had never thought to see on the ever stoic Freddy. He was afraid.

They took him in for emergency surgery as he went into a coma. It shook up the whole yard. Since the infected can live with HCV for decades, the end stages of the disease are a mystery to most. While only 2 percent of the general population have the disease, 12-35 percent of prisoners, depending on the state, have HCV, with California near the top at 34 percent (CDCP, 2013). The rumours ran the gamut, anything from a "liver transplant" to "he died". Then, about a week later, Freddy came back to the yard. So glad to see the old grouch, I almost cried. He looked like shit. His eyes had sunk into a skull attached to a pencil-thin neck. For a while, however, Freddy seemed to bounce back. Some of his old humour and sarcasm returned.

But Freddy's improvement did not last long. His liver gave out again in early December. They took him to a Reno hospital in what would be a last attempt to stave off death. The only thing that could have saved Freddy was a liver transplant.

When Freddy returned from the second surgery, I was determined to document his story. "If they got me eighteen months ago", he told me, "They probably could have saved me". Three of us sat at a table in the dayroom. Two of us listened intently. Interviewing a friend just before he died created a strange dynamic. Since I consider myself a writer, I had to put my money where my mouth is. As an activist and a jailhouse lawyer, I always take an aggressive stance in all my jailhouse journalism. This was different. I mainly listened as I took my notes. I was mad.

"By the time they did something, it was too late". There was no anger in his voice, only resignation more alarming than any of his rants. "When your ammonia levels are high", Freddy explained, "You are supposed to be on a strict diet".

The doctors at the Reno hospital could not believe the prison medical department simply left him untreated after his surgery. Complete inaction when a patient is screaming for treatment is unthinkable – and why so many suits have been filed. The Reno doctors had assumed that Freddy would be placed on a diet low in protein and sodium. The liver is an amazing organ, and stabilization opens the door for regeneration, treatment and perhaps experimentation. Diet alone can add months, or even years, to a dying patient's life. Inexcusable. "They killed me, bro", was Freddy's verdict.

An outlaw of the highest order, Freddy hated the government. At some point, he always expected the entire tough-on-crime movement to give way to economic collapse. He wanted to see a total fiscal meltdown lead to prison and sentencing reform. This tsunami of change, he opined, might even extend to an old career criminal like himself. At this moment in his criminal career, ever the anarchist, Freddy stayed true to form. "I cost them a couple hundred thousand dollars", Freddy bragged. "Good. I hope it bankrupts them. Every little bit helps".

I keep replaying that last conversation in my mind. Sometimes I even hear it in my sleep. When the ambulance came on the yard a few days later, Freddy's words immediately came back to me. In my gut, I knew they had come for my dying friend. All movement freezes when an ambulance comes into the yard. Hundreds of prisoners were seated silently on the yard. As the ambulance crew slowly brought him out on a gurney, the mood was bleak. We asked one of the guards about Freddy. "The old grouch told me to go to hell". We all laughed.

It was December 29, 2005. Freddy died that day, in the ambulance on the way to the hospital. Most of us remain shocked by how quickly the virus took Freddy. Just a few years ago, he played handball and worked out with men half his age. Now he is dead. Freddy might have deserved to be permanently separated from society for a life of crime, but he did not deserve a death sentence administered through medical neglect and incompetence.

Citing the sixty preventable deaths a year like Freddy's as the prompt, the CDCR's medical department has been in federal receivership since 2005 (Verdin, 2013). Four years later, a panel of federal judges placed a cap on the population in order to bring these murderous and unconstitutional conditions of medical and mental health into decent standards of care (ibid). The Supreme Court recently ruled in favour of the prisoner class, an unprecedented measure.

For Freddy, who died just shy of his fifty-fourth birthday, it does not matter. In all his layers of ugliness and imperfection, Freddy was a true American outlaw. He went out like he lived, breaking the law. A few months after he died, a package of legal paper arrived. A small load of heroin had been secreted in the documents addressed to him. In my mind, the missive came from the grave. Always the criminal, Freddy must have sent the shit from hell just to aggravate the guards. It is my story, and that is the way I choose to tell it.

POSTSCRIPT

Freddy's 2005 death illuminates many of the problems that continue to plague the carceral. A number of improvements made by the federal receiver did not impress the judiciary. In a landmark decision, the Supreme Court held the delivery system was impossible to improve due to overcrowding and ordered California to lower the population by roughly 40,000 prisoners by 2013 (Brown, 2011).

California is the epicentre of the tough-on-crime movement. The pendulum of national reformation that started swinging in the early to mid-2000s is now being pushed by steady pressure from the courts (Dey, 2006). A higher level of accountability, expediency and professionalism is noticeable, but the abundance of chronic care prisoners, many of whom are elderly and doing life, forces medical to run almost twenty-four hours a day in Soledad (Dey, 2007; Dey, 2010).

This type of nonstop health care is draining correction's budget in a state on the brink of fiscal disaster (Brown, 2011). California barely has money to properly fund education and provide basic social services, let alone build more prisons and continue to house prisoners all over the country. By handing California a solution on a silver platter, alternatives to the $10 billion nightmare of mindless incarceration can be developed.

California is now on a federal clock – and it is ticking. Major reforms matched by cutting-edge rehabilitative programming will have to be embraced to maintain the reductions. Freddy was right about economic collapse fuelling reform. The death of guys like him and depressing conditions that lead to suicide are now combined with the overriding need for fiscal constraint. It is a perfect storm – and may even result in lasting change.

REFERENCES

Brown v. Plata (2011) 563 U.S. ___ [Slip Opinion, pp. 1-52].

Center for Disease Control and Prevention (2013) "Correctional Facilities and Viral Hepatitis" – May 28. Retrieved from http://www.cdc.gov/hepatitis/Settings/corrections.htm.

Dey, Eugene (2010) "Soapbox: Health Care For Elderly Inmates Costly", *The Salinas Californian* – May 19.

Dey, Eugene (2007) "Hepatitis C and the California Prisoner", *Journal of Prisoners on Prisons*, 16(2): 53-58.

Dey, Eugene (2006) "The Pendulum of Change and California's Three Strikes Law", *Journal of Prisoners on Prisons*, 15(1): 42-52.

Verdin, Tom (2013) "California Prison Population Cap Removal Denied By Federal Judicial Panel", *Huffington Post* – April 11. Retrieved from http://www.huffingtonpost.com/2013/04/12/california-prison-population-cap_n_3070831.html.

ABOUT THE AUTHOR

Eugene Dey is a former prisoner, regular *JPP* contributor and member of the Editorial Board. As a recipient of California's notorious three strikes and you're out sentencing law, Eugene spent 15 years in prison advocating through a multitude of litigious and literary endeavours. However, a shift in penal policy caused by landmark litigation in the California criminal justice system led to a multitude of changes, including three strikes being amended by the voters in 2012. As a result, Eugene is among three strikers who have been released from prison and continues his work through his firm Outside Solutions.

Eugene Dey
Outside Solutions
P.O. Box 7095
Soledad, CA 95621
USA

outsidesolutions.ed@gmail.com

How One Idea Almost Became Law:
A Case Study
Jon Marc Taylor

During the summer of 1996, I had an epiphany. If the State of Missouri received $3 million in rebates (unknown at the time to rise shortly thereafter to $10 million per annum) from the MCI-WORLDCOM Inmate Phone System contract, why not use that money to replace the Pell Grants, a post-secondary education subsidy program that prisoners had been excluded from the year before by a myopic Congress? The following case study chronicles the step-by-step efforts made to transform the concept into legislative reality, as well as some of the challenges we faced.

THE PROCESS

The first step was to draft a white paper of the concept to communicate the idea to a larger audience, and then to have the article published for wider dissemination. "Calling for Sheepskins" was prominently published in the Winter 1996-1997 issue of the *Cry Justice Journal*[1]:

> In 1994, two related yet apparently unassociated events occurred in Missouri prisons. First, all college programs were closed down. Second, the State General Fund received nearly three million dollars in rebates from the MCI Corporation. [...]

> For the past half-century, poll after poll has shown public support for "treating" or "rehabilitating" those incarcerated, in order that they would not return to crime when released. Even one of the main sponsors of the legislation mounted to discontinue prisoners' eligibility for Pell Grants, Representative Bart Gordon [D–Tennessee], was not opposed to prisoners' higher education. The problem, he stated, was "not whether prisoners should be educated, but whether Pell Grants are an appropriate vehicle to do that." Since federal funds to finance college curriculum in Missouri prisons are no longer available, a new funding source needs to be found. A primary criticism of prisoners receiving Pell Grants was concern over the use of tax dollars to pay for inmates' educations, which was viewed by some to be "rewarding" criminal behaviour. In today's climate of tight state budgets, and struggles to house and feed ever-expanding prison populations, finding

state tax money to reinstate higher education for people who have been convicted seems a fruitless proposition. [...] Legislation should be introduced that would direct revenue from the inmate phone system into the inmate canteen fund, specifically earmarked to fund post-secondary education. The canteen fund could mirror the formula of Pell Grants, matching the amount awarded with the amount a prisoner would have received if eligible for the Pell program. [...]

If this legislation were passed, each time someone accepted a call from a prisoner, they would be helping to send one through college. In this small way they would be enriching many futures by increasing the likelihood that prisoners will be successfully rehabilitated, thus making their own neighbourhoods safer for everyone's children.

The article was well received with copies distributed well beyond the subscription base of the *Cry Justice Journal*. The second step was to craft a lobbying strategy to have legislation introduced and passed. This required the creation of a proposal kit, recruiting a lobbyist, and targeting likely representatives to support the measure. The *Proposal for the Recommencement of Post-Secondary Education Opportunities in Missouri Prisons* kit was compiled and produced with the resources we had available at the prison.[2] It consisted of four sections from the "Sheepskins" article, and half a dozen related pieces from substantial publications.[3] As for a lobbyist, we lucked out with a sweet, physically frail, elderly Catholic nun with a beauteous smile of an angel and the heart of a lioness: Sister Ruth Heaney, the Mother Teresa of Missouri prisoners.[4] She knew the legislators, had periodically lobbied from capitol office to office for decades, and most of all, knew how the "game was played". She began contacting the senators[5] that introduced the bipartisan sponsored Senate Bill 336[6] and (22 co-sponsoring) representatives of House Bill 481[7] in the 89th General Assembly during the first weeks of 1997.

The next step was to generate support for the bills. The state Coordinating Board for Higher Education provided a roster of all the college presidents. Sixty personalized form letters were then sent out to these administrators in mid-March, 1997. An excerpted example of which follows:

This letter is in regards to pending House Bill No. 481 and Senate Bill 336, which would direct the rebate commission from the MDOC Inmate

Phone-MCI contract to fund post-secondary education opportunities for the state's prisoners. The multi-year contract guarantees a minimum of $10 million a year in rebates from this program. Instead of being added to the state general revenue, these funds could be invested in Missouri institutions of higher education.

Enclosed are copies of the legislation, topic broadsheets relating to the issue, and two short articles concerning the issue of prisoner higher education, previously funded by the federal Pell Grants. These documents will provide you with the necessary background to evaluate the efficacy of the situation. [...]

I strongly urge you to promptly contact your district's representative and senator, voicing your support for this legislation. As well, I suggest contacting the legislations' sponsors, advising them of your support and actions. Time is of the essence. Delays threaten the success of this most positive endeavour. [...]

Over the following weeks, several college presidents replied and included copies of their correspondence to their respective representatives. A sampling of these responses is as follows:

Thank you for your letter [...] alerting me to pending House Bill 481 and Senate Bill 336. I have spoken with lobbyists in Jefferson City and indicated my support for these bills. We will do what we can to encourage passage so as to provide educational opportunities for prison inmates.

Melvin George, Interim President (3-25-97)

Some educators responded by lobbying their representatives. For instance:

Dear Senator Edward Quick,

I strongly urge your support for Senate Bill #336 that would fund post-secondary education for inmates. [...] This Missouri Bill probably won't affect Park College, because the state prisons in Missouri had worked with nearby state universities. However, I wanted to be certain you knew that I strongly support prison degree completion programs. I will happily testify at any hearing as an expert witness, or do whatever else I can.

[Signed] Don Bracken, President, Park College (3-24-97)

Seeking a "hook" or wedge issue with which to leverage the concept with the legislature, propitiously (or maybe Divinely) Sister Ruth brought in the March 1996 article "It's our Christian duty to educate prisoners" from *U.S. Catholic,* which reported that the magazine's survey showed overwhelming support for sponsoring prison-based college programs. Obtaining a list of the legislators of the Catholic faith (a third of the sitting body), a lobbying packet was sent in April 1997 that detailed the following[8]:

> This letter is in regards to HB 481 & SB 336 concerning the refinancing of state prisoners' post-secondary educational opportunities via **non-taxpayer dollars**. The legislation would redirect the rebate commission from the MCI-Inmate Phone System contract from the state general fund to instead refinance post-secondary opportunities that were once supported by federal Pell Grants. [...]

> Beyond the economic and social rationales for providing Post-Secondary Correctional Education (PSCE) opportunities, there is a moral imperative in doing so. Enclosed, among other fact sheets on this issue, is an article from *U.S. Catholic* magazine. Besides chronicling the value of PSCE programs and the Pell Grant controversy, the piece reports on a representative readership sample surveying their opinions on the issue. I would like to share some of those results with this letter. [...]

One response to this mailing was from Representative Norman Sheldon (4-29-97) stating that he "agree[d] with the concept of [my] letter and that PSCF is the best rehabilitative tool that can be offered as of today".

WELTPOLITICK

Support for the legislation came from groups both in and outside of the state. The Public Policy Committee of the Missouri Catholic Conference (MCC) endorsed the bills.[9] Julie Stewart, the president of the Washington-based Families Against Mandatory Minimums (FAMM) Foundation, offered to do whatever they could to support passage, commenting that the proposal was a "brilliant" idea and that was a concept her organization would "like to pursue with other states and maybe federally".[10] Missouri Citizens United for the Rehabilitation Errants (MO-CURE) published notice of the bills in their newsletter as well. The Correctional Education Association wished us "good luck with the bill!" and requested progress updates.

As with the prisoner-student Pell Grant eligibility being a controversial issue in the 1980s and 1990s, back room *weltpolitick* machinations influenced events around the efforts made to refinance education for prisoners. While passing out of the Senate Committee, the Bill 481 failed in its House Committee in 1997. Not only had the MDOC curiously failed to support the bills,[11] but an illuminating incident also occurred in the capitol moments after the House Committee's vote. The following incident was relayed by Sister Ruth, as told to her by the representative involved. In an initial perceived-to-be, off-the-cuff confiding to one of the co-sponsoring legislators, the MDOC director cryptically commented, "It's too much money". Curiosity piqued, and acting upon a hunch, the freshman representative acquired a copy of the new phone contract and learned that the annual rebate had grown to a guaranteed minimum of $10 million a year. Moreover, with the perpetual growth in the state's penal population, the projected rebate to the state's general revenue fund over the five-year life of the contract exceeded $60 million!

Given that crucial piece of information, it became clear that if the "Sheepskins" legislation had been passed, the state would not only be denied tens of millions of dollars in non-taxed revenue, but prisoners would have the opportunity to earn fully-subsidized college educations. To some politicians the loss of the indirectly levied revenue traded for higher education to prisoners would be unpalatable. The rationale be damned! That seemingly off-the-cuff remark, lobbed over the shoulder in a "chance passing" in a capitol building stairwell, of "It's too much money", now made sense. Or as a representative who speciously justified his negative vote on HB 481 reasoned:

> My philosophical problem with this bill is the funding of post-secondary education for our convicted felons. As soon as we fully fund college educations for all of Missouri's high school graduates [ignoring the fact that prisoners' collect phone calls would be funding their own education], I will reconsider my position [i.e., as in, when this improbable prerequisite criteria is met]. I cannot, in good conscience [or by logic or fairness; i.e., besides Pell Grants, prisoners are statutorily excluded in state and federal levels from student loans and state higher education grants], give to a convicted felon, that which we cannot give to the public at large.

Despite the initial defeat, sponsoring legislators in both chambers expressed more confidence, with the experience gained from the previous session, in regards to passing the enabling legislation. Strategies were refined, coalitions constructed and reinforced, and resources marshalled. Realistically, we had been wildly successful in advancing our vision so far at a rapid pace. After all, less than 2 percent of all bills submitted in any given session ever make it to the Governor's desk for signing. Most do not even garner a committee hearing, much less a vote. In short, we were hyped at the prospects for the following session. However, it was at this point that the opponents of the measure instituted the most Machiavellian of actions to silence me.

REPERCUSSIONS

In June of 1997, one week after my promotion to the most reasonable prisoner position in the Missouri Department of Corrections, Resident Director of the Center of Braille and Narration Production, I was summarily transferred to the newest maximum-security, death-fenced enclosed penitentiary in the state's far northwest corner. While a shock, the transfer was not a total surprise. I knew that I had been picked up on the radar of those opposing the legislation.[12]

For the preceding years (out of my eighteen years of incarceration), I had survived in the 160-year-old Missouri State Prison[13] – recently, if not magically, re-christened the Jefferson City Correctional Center – with only a single, very minor rule violation blotting my institutional conduct record. Moreover, I was an active board member of the Charitable Campaign Committee, which was responsible for collecting the prison's aluminium soda cans for recycling, raising over $10,000 during my tenure for donation to area food banks. Additionally, I served as the media liaison for the Substance Abuse Advisory Committee, arranging print and broadcast coverage of several of the group's more beneficial programs, as well as those of other groups. The superintendent once commented, after watching the $3,000 donation ceremony filmed by two television stations, that I was helping to give the public a non-stereotypical view of convicts.[14] During all of this, I had also continued with my collegiate distance education pursuits.

My greatest achievement, however, had been to advance from narrator to narration supervisor to resident director of the Center for Braille and Narration Production. The CBNP is the oldest and most prolific prison-based program of its type in the country. The indirectly-supervised resident director is responsible for overseeing $50,000 in computer, printer, recording and duplicating equipment with annual billings exceeding $70,000, realizing a ten-fold plus multiple value in services delivered to those physically less fortunate.[15]

All of this was in my favour, and yet I was chosen to be shipped out, ahead of over 700 similarly eligible prisoners to complete the human consignment filling the newly opened prison. The day of my transfer, I received a phone call in my fifth floor office with a view of the state's shining capitol dome visible over the prisoner-built wall. The high-ranking prison administrator on the other end of the line commiserated with me over the fact that there was nothing to be done to stop the transfer. The order, he advised, had originated from the central office, and not at the prison's recommendation. "Your editorial and legislative activism," he ponderously stated, "had disturbed the status quo of the powers that be, and they want you as far from the capital as possible. Crossroads [the new prison] is about as far away as you can get".[16]

THE END OF THE LINE

One week after my arrival at the new prison, I was rousted at midnight by three officers in my cell. In a quick series of moves during an ordered strip search, I was handcuffed, thrown into isolation (aka "the hole"), and charged with assault on staff and possession of marijuana. Even though the reporting sergeant admitted I had fully cooperated with all his orders, that I was not belligerent or resistive, and that I had not touched him, I was still found guilty of assault of staff, though not of possession. I was sentenced to one year in the hole with referral for criminal prosecution to boot.

Within days of starting my sojourn in the hole, I began receiving letters from the capitol. One of the co-sponsoring state representatives, Vicky Riback Wilson, wrote on July 30, 1997, confiding she had "heard" that I had been transferred and of her intent to re-file education funding legislation. "In addition to the supportive organizations you mentioned in your letter", she continued, "I have spoken to people from community colleges – Moberly, Three Rivers – Lincoln University, and vocational programs. I think there is a strong coalition of supporters; however, they need to be organized and mobilized. I will check with Senator Flotron (R) so we can coordinate our efforts".

The next day, Senator Franc Flotron's letter of July 22, 1997, arrived. He wrote:

The Senate version was voted 'Do Pass' in committee, but never was turned
in for full Senate consideration...this will be on my list for submission
[for next year's session]. My advice would be to continue working on the
implementation material.

Then the follow-up letter from Representative Norman Sheldon – one of the
sixty "Catholic" mailings – was shoved under the solid steel isolation door:

Thank you for writing me an informed and interesting letter concerning
HB 481. The bad news is that the bill did not make it out of the Correctional
and State Institutions Committee...I agree with the concept of your letter
and that PGCE is the best rehabilitative tool that can be offered today.
(June 29, 1997) [The chronologically reverse order of the letters' receipt
is an example of the vagaries of prisoner mail delivery].

Entombed in the hole with all my resources in storage, I was now powerless
to offer my knowledge, experience and support. I had been silenced. At
least that was what the intended endeavour the state was to effect.

By the end of the year, working through the good auspices of Sister
Ruth, "Calling for Sheepskins" was reprinted in the *Cry Justice Journal*,
resurrecting the issue with a broader yet targeted audience. Thus, buried
in the hole, denied access to all but a pencil and legal pad, limited to only
handwritten correspondence for communication, I had found a way to
energize the fight enlisting numerous supporters.

Days after the New Year commenced, Representative Vicky Riback
Wilson wrote: "Thank you for informing me of the statistics of recidivism
rates. [...] I appreciate your continued activism on this issue" (January 5,
1998). On January 15, 1998, House Bill 1372 was submitted for consideration.
A month later, Representative Wilson updated me on the events. "As you
suggested", she wrote, "Representative Troupe and I discussed lowering the
percentage of funds available for education to 25. However, we decided to
start with the whole amount since it would be easier to reduce it later rather
than increase it" (February 17, 1998). Although the bill eventually advanced
further in the committee process, with the chairman now supporting the
legislation, it failed to be scheduled for a full floor vote.

Concomitantly, the repercussions continued. Two days before Christmas
1997, I was transported to the county seat and arraigned on felony charges

of Class B assault and Class C possession of 0.18 grams of marijuana (i.e. less than half the weight of a disposable packet of pepper). The initial plea bargain offer was for 20 years to run consecutively (a.k.a. "wild") to my current sentence. Dismissing the Public Pretender, cashing in a mutual fund I had been investing in for a decade as my eventual "gate money", I hired a notoriously rabid attorney known as the "Matlock of Missouri". However, by highlighting the availability of assets, the state Attorney General correspondingly filed an incarceration reimbursement forfeiture action against me, eventually seizing the remainder of my hard-earned, carefully invested and long-hoarded savings. The filing and timing of the state's civil action seems more than a mite coincidental.[17]

By the summer of 1998, I had won my grievance appeal, having the director herself dismiss my staff assault violation (only after serving ten months of a year-long sanction though). The criminal case was dismissed a week before trial, based primarily on my earlier filed *pro se* motions requesting an in-camera review of the charging officer's personnel file and chain of evidence challenge regarding the alleged marijuana (i.e. it had disappeared somewhere along the way – imagine that). Moreover, we now had irrefutable evidence of forgery with conspiracy implications regarding the original Conduct Violation charging form. The *pièce de résistance* in all of this being the charging sergeant's demotion and his subsequent dismissal with cause, whereupon he was unable to obtain similar employment in other correctional systems.

Yet, the latest house bill had failed, again. With further changes in the phone contract system, thankfully eliminating the rebate and thus lowering overall charges, my transfer from one prison to another, ten months in the hole on trumped up charges, and lack of solid organizational support, I was unable to prosecute the campaign as effectively as I had been able to the previous year. The concerted multi-dimensional assaults orchestrated by the nebulous "powers that be" had achieved their assumed intent of effectively removing me from the lobbying process.

If we had been able to conduct an education and lobbying campaign via the prison branches of the National Association for the Advancement of Coloured People (MO-CURE), Families Against Mandatory Minimums (FAMM) and Missouri Association of Social Workers (MASW), these significant resources could then have likely built upon the group work already laid, making a major push for the legislation's passage. If not for passage of the specific legislation, then for serious debate regarding the lack of higher education opportunities in the state's prisons. As it was, and continues to this day, there is virtually no legislative cognizance of the supreme value and corresponding paucity of correctional education in the Show-Me State.[18] In fact, in 2005, all education programs (i.e. remaining Adult Basic Education and General Equivalency Diploma) were removed from three of the state's maximum-security prisons, leaving them no educational or vocational training programs at all.

The swan song of the "Sheepskins" legislation occurred in 1999, with the submission of yet another bill. In my admittedly half-hearted efforts to support, the speaker of the house responded to my inquiry:

> A particular piece of legislation that accomplishes your concern has been introduced by Representative Quincy Troupe, Vicki Riback Wilson, Mike Schilling, Bill Gratz, Wayne Crumo, Sam Leake, and Amber Boykins and referred to the House Committee on Correctional and State Institutions. HB 601 requires up to 40% of any profits made by the state from long distance calls be placed in the telephone-education fund. The money from this fund is used for the post-secondary education of inmates (February 22, 1999).

This bill, too, failed to pass.

ANALYSIS

This case study chronicles on the one hand the failure to have legislation passed into law, and on the other it demonstrates what one little old lady, a prisoner and a few friends donating stamps can accomplish with a viable idea, detailed planning, and perseverance in execution in the pursuit of a dream.

The errors in our strategy in retrospect were committed in ignorance, procedural oversight and lack of organization resources. First, we should have drafted the specific legislation ourselves and submitted it to the sponsoring legislators. This way both bills would have been worded identically, thus eliminating the necessity of the language reconciliation procedure between the chambers' bills if they had been passed.

Second, as much as we tried to educate the legislators on the issue, imparting a more profound analysis might have made a difference. We needed more lobbyists and more face time in Q & A debate not only with supporters, but more so with opponents. We needed to push for committee hearings on the legislation and then prepare ourselves to provide informed testimony.

Third, we needed to organize an even greater "voter" lobbying campaign encompassing endorsement letters, emails and phone calls to legislators' offices. On issues such as this, half a dozen to ten contacts on a specific bill would be unusual, and thus attentive of larger support. Politicians are sensitive to future votes. Even if a particular legislator disagrees with the pending bill, their response in itself is informative, offering opportunities for well-crafted rebuttals to stated objections, and thus hopefully converting them to allies. And if not so persuaded, they identify themselves as those to campaign against in the subsequent election.

Finally, we needed more resources and especially organizational allies. This requires a lot of effort, negotiation and long-term planning. At times, it can seem like trying to herd cats! But together, with those of us on the inside working with those who advocate for a more inclusive and rehabilitative correctional system from the outside, effective legislative conditions can be built.[19] It is up to *us* to accomplish such achievements.

AFTERWORD

This article, as well as the majority published herein over the past twenty-five years, would only have found voice in the *Journal of Prisoners on Prisons (JPP)*. The audacity of the founding editors to create an academic standard, peer-reviewed periodical for prisoners' research, opinions, and insights of those from within the gulag archipelago of the prison-industrial complex was tantamount of the highest hubris prevailing against the *zeitgeist* of the era. The perseverance of the subsequent editorial boards has been in unvarnished perpetual support pursuing intellectual inquiry within the expansively viewed academy in philosophical concurrence to the *Pedagogy of the Oppressed*. Without these essentially unknown folks of liberal morality, academic ethics and good will, my voice and the value of that voice as well as hundreds of other prisoners' voices over the years would have never been heard, much less recorded and added to the common body of knowledge.

Yet, even this periodical in its loving process of production, exemplifies the very need for the *JPP*. Of all the academic journals my work has been published by, the journal's blind, peer-reviewed process has been the most professional in format and incisive in assisting me to produce the best of my submitted work. In this process, however, the gulf of demarcation between the free and the imprisoned reveal itself.

I am immensely grateful to the anonymous reviewers of this article's manuscript. It is a better, more coherent piece because of their insightful comments and suggestions. From their comments I can assume they are professional academics with experience in the related fields of criminology and criminal justice. Their comments also reveal the disconnect between even the best educated of our ensconced worlds and those of us in the steel cages we actually struggle to survive in.

One reviewer wrote that the only question they had concerning the piece was that "the body of the narrative is very critical of the correctional system's efforts to silence and suppress the author's activity around legislative change and making education accessible to prisoners, while the conclusion's analysis focuses solely on how the campaign could have been strengthened on the part of the organizers". My initial response to such was "well, like, duh". That is the purpose of the piece. It is what transpired: the good, the bad, and the ugly. My goal is to chronicle this history, and to offer a template of how others may be able to adapt efforts to create change from within. For me this has always been a mission facet of *JPP*.

Another reviewer comment concerned the degree to which the piece contributed to the literature. They freely admitted they were unfamiliar with the "existing literature on political organizing inside prisons" (and ensuing state repression), or access on education for prisoners in the U.S. My response to this was that neither am I familiar with such literature, other than spotty, circumstantial exposure to such. Rarely, and then only briefly mentioned, is such information cited in the mainstream texts and journals. It is another reason I wrote the article.

As to the publication decision, one reviewer's comment was to question if the author's mention of his institutional charges and transfer were "pertinent to the larger narrative and commentary". My response to this is that it has been my perception that all of this had a direct causal relationship. If I had not been an "uppity inmate" not knowing my place in the scheme of things in the status quo, I would most likely never have been transferred and "free cased" with the guard assault and ridiculous possession charges. Moreover, those charges if enforced would have essentially meant I would never be released from prison. So, yes, I have visceral as well as intellectual reasons for believing the comprehensive narrative is critical to the comprehension of the piece's narrative.

The reviewer's comments also reminded me of my American parochialism, and the necessity to write for the international audience that *JPP* serves. The reviewers also suggested a comprehensive reading list of related materials as being beneficial.[20] It sure would be. Part of the purpose of this piece is to chronicle the experience and by doing so highlight the isolation prisoners and even activists endure in their efforts to affect change. The reviewer's comments also suggest a disconnect between the academic world with an abundance of immediate research resources and that of prisoners' with the description of extreme paucity of such being a gross understatement.

Again this reinforces the need for the great service *JPP* provides to the common body of knowledge to record such experiences. Without the extensive library that *JPP* has now published, this voice and hundreds of others with stories and views to tell would have been lonely shouts into the vastness of state sponsored repression. This forum is more relevant than ever, and needs to be read by a much wider audience. It should be part of every criminal justice major's supplemental reading list, if not part of a course curriculum in corrections.

ENDNOTES

[1] The *Cry Justice Journal* is published by the New Life Evangelical Center of Larry Rice Ministries. The publication had a circa print distribution of 10,000, with extensive institutional pass-along readership. A decade later, the publication was banned from the state's prisons, while it is now wholly published online. The article was also published, under the title of "Dialing for Diplomas", as a two-part series in the March and April 1997 issues of *Justicia*.

[2] At the time, I worked as the Narration Supervisor in the Center for Braille & Narration Production (CBNP) at the Jefferson City Correctional Center, which was located four blocks from the capitol building. The CBNP was a 20-man operation contracted by the state's Bureau of the Blind which we programmed Braille transcribing computers, having the output double-sided impact printed, collated and bound; narrated books onto cassette tapes, duplicated and Braille labelled; and scanned or input keyed, edited and produced large print orders. In 1996, the CBNP narrated 65,000 pages of text, transcribed over 70,000 pages of Braille and formatted 80,000 pages of large print documents, providing over $1 million in market-rate services for the visually impaired citizens of the state. I chronicle this environmentally unique

work assignment, because it provided access to desktop publishing equipment and spiral binding facilities that are generally not directly available to prison populations. Thus, I was able to professionally produce twenty-five, 100-page briefing manuals for our lobbyist's targeted use.

3 **TABLE OF CONTENTS:**

I. Proposal Article: "Calling for Sheepskins in Missouri Prisons". The Golden Rule of Advocacy

II. "Truth about prisons could change things". *National Catholic Reporter* (July 26, 1996)

"Prison Economics: Reality Bites". *Justicia* (July-August, 1996)

III. "There ought to Be a Law (but Not This Crime Bill)". *The New York Times* (August 24, 1994)

"It's our Christian duty to educate prisoners". *U.S. Catholic* (March 1996)

"Deny Pell Grants to Prisoners? That Would be a Crime". *Criminal Justice* (Summer 1994)

IV. "Post-Secondary Correctional Education: An Evaluation of Effectiveness and Efficiency". *Journal of Correctional Education* (September 1992)

"Should Prisoners Have Access to Collegiate Education? A Policy Issue". *Educational Policy* (September 1994)

4 A pioneer in the Catholic Worker movement, a widow since 1950 and founding member of the Missouri Commission on Human Rights in 1957, she became Benedictine in 1974, after her six children were raised. Sister Ruth invested decades in daily visits to Missouri prisons, bringing her endless agape to thousands, and conducting Alternatives to Violence and Positive Mental Attitude workshops, while leading weekly ecumenical Journey in Faith discussion groups, which is where I first encountered her. She helped establish Agape House, a hostel in the capital where people visiting imprisoned loved ones could economically spend the night. In 2005, Sister Ruth received the Missouri Association for Social Welfare Humanitarian Award. In her acceptance speech, she remarked that "prisons are places of structured dehumanization. People in prison live under constant deprivation of things people really need, as well as humiliation around the clock". Over her ministry, she was "permanently" kicked out of Missouri prisons four times. By 2002, though, the administration and prisoners celebrated Sister Ruth Heaney day and established an award in her honor for exceptional volunteer services to penal populations. This blessed woman of infinite spiritual joy passed away in 2006, having more than any other human being positively affected generations of Missouri prisoners. Sister Ruth is dearly missed.

5 One was a childhood friend of an associate of mine at the prison and activist in many community programs. This prisoner (co-founder of the MDOC's immensely successful Intensive Therapeutic Community program) provided an introductory/ endorsement letter to the respected conservative politician that I believe was crucial in convincing the senator not only to co-sponsor the bill, but also to recruit a bi-partisan co-sponsor. The important facet in this story is that such familial and friendly relationships between prisoners and the various elements in the establishment exist in every system. Focused utilization of such contact can mean the difference between fair consideration of proposals and the stonewalling of legislation.

[6] (SB 336) **AN ACT** – To amend chapter 217, RSMO, by adding thereto one new section relating to offender education.

    1. The department shall establish a fund to be known as the "Post-Secondary Education Fund" to assist offenders who want to pursue post-secondary education.

    2. The department shall deposit all profits collected from the operation of the inmate phone system into the post-secondary education fund. The monies in the fund shall not revert to be transferred to general revenue, notwithstanding the provisions of section 33.090, RSMO, to the contrary. The department shall maintain accurate records of the amount of monies in the post-secondary education fund and shall allocate monies from the fund to each correctional facility as needed.

[7] (HB 481) **AN ACT** – Relating to education for inmates.

    Section 1. Any profits received by the state from long distance calls made in facilities of the department of corrections shall be transferred to the director of revenue to be deposited in the "Telephone Education Fund" which is hereby created in the state treasury. Moneys in this fund shall be available, subject to appropriation, to be used for inmates' post-secondary education, in any format, offered by educational institutions which are accredited in Missouri.

[8] Collectively, over 150 pieces of correspondence were posted relating to the 1997 legislative efforts. Even with the relative premium wages earned at the CBNP, this was a substantial personal expense. To utilize the CBNP production facilities, I had briefed an entire staff, which had unanimously voted to support the project. This also included their donations of postage. I mention this seemingly trivial aspect because efficient and creative use of limited resources is critical for prisoner activists. Enlisting allies for brain storming sessions, moral courage, and access to shared assets from contacts to copying and typing to even stamps can quite likely make the difference between a grandiose idea and realistic shot at changing a small part of the world we inhabit.

[9] Readership survey results from the March 1996 issue of *U.S. Catholic*:

    * "Educating prisoners is one good way to reduce the number of criminals returning to prison". **91% AGREE**

    * "Prisoners gave up their right to an education when they committed their crime". **87% DISAGREE**

    * "It makes good social and economic sense to put prisoners' time to good use by giving them an education". **87% AGREE**

    * "Providing education for prisoners will make prison less of a deterrent". **82% DISAGREE**

    * "Funds for education should go prisoners of all ages". **87% AGREE**

    * "I believe it's our Christian duty to educate prisoners". **84% AGREE**

[10] MCC's April 1997 newsletter, *Good News*, ran the column "Senate Committee approves funds to educate inmates". The story detailed, "In testimony to the Committee Senator Flotron noted this would be an appropriate way to fund college programs because the money is generated from inmate families rather than State funds. Studies show that inmates receiving college education have a lower recidivism rate than other inmates" (p. 3).

[11] In a matter of conjecture, I have pondered why a bureaucrat would not support an off-appropriation $10 million budget increase. The director was the former deputy director of NY-DOC and had overseen that state's then nationally exceptional PSCE

program, and thus knew the programmatic and rehabilitative value of the opportunity. Due to supplant/supplement budgetary games played during her administration of the MO-DOC, Missouri prisoners had been among those in a handful of states who had lost the Pell Grant eligibility a year before than the blanket national expulsion. This new funding source would, in turn, provide a five-fold (500%) increase in post-secondary funding over what was received the last year the state's prisoner students had received in Pell Grant financing. This non-direct tax generated funding would provide an Ivy League-level of PSCE programming. Why would a DOC director and a professional bureaucrat turn down such "free" largesse? My theory is that a *sub rosa* political deal was made. What the specific arrangements for *quid pro quo* are unknown, but the legislature's powers that be did not want to give up these multi-millions in non-levied dollars. Why else would such an experienced corrections professional abandon the opportunity to creatively finance the premiere Post-Secondary Correctional Education program in the nation? Why indeed.

12 A few weeks after the second mass mailing, by happenstance (but perhaps by arranged coincidence in retrospection) I crossed paths with one of the prison's internal investigators. We had never interacted. Not even knowing his name, but nonetheless thoroughly aware of who he was, we exchanged polite nods as we awaited the central wheelhouse to open a gate. Out of the blue, he observed, "those were a lot of letters that went out to the legislature." Turning to look up at this gargantuan man, I replied, "Yes, there were many". Since these had been sent to public officials, I was able to post them in sealed envelopes, as opposed to unsealed and searchable ones as policy dictated for general correspondence. I had no illusions that the prison had not surreptitiously opened at least some of the sixty to learn what was being sent out. At the time, I gave the chance encounter no serious consideration that the administration would read the contents, because it was similar to what I had openly sent to the college presidents a few weeks earlier. In a (later perceived as chilling) parting shot, he quipped, "Go with God". This was a reference to the "Catholic" nature of the mailing, letting me know that they had indeed read the mailings. It was a message. The system made sure I knew that they knew what I was doing. And later with my transfer and subsequently arranged nightmare, perhaps I should have less hubris. Then again, by that time, it was already too late – and like Paul Newman's character of *Cool Hand Luke*, I hate being bullied by the system.

13 See ibid.

14 The Missouri State Penitentiary was once labelled "the Bloodiest 54-Acres in America". Though these lurid times had passed before my transfer there, "The Walls" were nonetheless a hardcore place to do time.

15 At the time, I took that as a compliment. Soon thereafter, however, I had cause to reason otherwise. Ironically, because of my apparent media aplomb, the superintendent requested that I interview him for the closed-circuit channel ("Jefftown"), regarding his tour of the soon to be opened Crossroads Correctional Center. A few months later, I received my own on-going tour of this patch of Missouri.

16 He actually talked like this. He was one of the most equitable penal administrators I have ever met. If he could be sold on the value of a program and an operationally logical outline, he would facilitate its enactment. Because he was viewed as too "pro-prisoner", by the same "powers that be" no less, he was never promoted higher

than deputy superintendent. Never thought I would say this about a "screw", but I long for the proverbial good old days of his "correctional administration".

[17] In clear violation of constitutional *ex post facto* protections (the seizure law had been passed eight years after my conviction), the courts ruled in the state's favour and seized assets. Two years later, after receiving a publisher's $1500 reprint rights check, the Attorney General filed another action. This time in *pro se* filings I succeeded in having the suit dismissed as insufficient in meeting the statutory criteria. A year later, the Attorney General flew an assistant to Maine to serve filings on the publisher of the first two editions of my book, *The Prisoners' Guerrilla Handbook to Correspondence Programs in the United States & Canada* (a project I had also initiated while in the hole on the trumped-up guard-assault charges). That case, too, was summarily dismissed. In 2007, the Attorney General, utilizing evolving legal interpretations and strategy froze my institutional account for over a year, garnishing 90 percent of all income in perpetuity of my incarceration, with the intentions of garnishing 20 percent of my post-release income until the $400,000 of the then estimated cost of my incarceration, if it was held the entire length of sentence, was collected. With the deft assistance of the only attorney in the state with experience regarding this particular statute, all by the initial proceedings were dismissed, and all assets except the initial forfeiture were returned in 2009, eleven years after the original filing.

[18] Missouri's state nickname, like the "Golden State" is California's.

[19] An absolutely intriguing story expanding upon this concept is told in Jamie Pissonnette's *When the Prisoners Ran Walpole: A True Story in the Movement for Prisoner Abolition.*

[20] One reviewer's suggested reading is Munn, Melissa and Chris Bruckert. (2010) "Beyond Conceptual Ambiguity: Exemplifying the 'Resistance Pyramid Through the Reflections of (Ex)Prisoners' Agency", *Qualitative Sociology Review*, 6(2): 137-145.

ABOUT THE AUTHOR

Jon Marc Taylor, PhD, has been a prisoner for the past 30 years and has received *The Nation* / I.F. Stone and Robert F. Kennedy Journalism awards for his reporting on correctional issues. In 1989, Taylor's first piece in the *Journal of Prisoners on Prisons*, "The Economics of Educational Rehabilitation", appeared in Volume 2(1).

Prison Literacy:
Light in a Dark Place
Colin McGregor

T he world of prison is largely without trees. Doubtless trees pose some sort of security risk, perhaps providing places where people can hide or hide their drugs. But one young maple, thirty feet tall, stands alone in a corner of our gardens, near where the barbed wire fencing meets the world outside our reach. Every week I sit under that tree, at a picnic table, with another prisoner. Marven Cain is 65. He has run companies, was married twice, and fathered several children, some late in life. But he cannot read a word. We sit and we read. He always insists on sitting under that lonely maple. He says it is his lucky tree. It is where he first began to make out words.

Looking for causes of crime? There is no more direct statistical link than that between illiteracy and criminal activity. Calamai (1987) found only one out of twenty-five federal prisoners are functionally illiterate in both of Canada's official languages. Two decades later, prisoners are still "three times as likely as the general population to have literacy problems" (Movement for Canadian Literacy, 2003, p. 6). Illiteracy engenders frustration. People cannot achieve what they want or earn what they think they deserve. They lash out. They steal. They hit. They drink and take drugs. *Le décrochage scolaire* and crimes are Siamese twins.

An illiterate prisoner cannot read the judge's decision that sent him to prison or the correctional evaluations that will determine if and when he is ever released. We have long hours to ourselves in a cell. Reading fills time with mental journeys. It is a way to escape mentally. The ancient Romans called the world of writing "The Land of Shadows". For most prisoners, this is a sadly inaccessible place.

My 65-year-old friend wants to read to his kids and his grandkids when he gets out. I have a college education. I was once a writer and a teacher before the system put me here. I am no humanitarian; I am just bored and want to use my training. That is why we sit under his lucky tree. Marven haltingly makes out a sentence. He looks up at the leaves, starting to turn auburn colours and punches at the air. "Thank you, Lord", he says in a whisper. "I didn't think I could ever read". I detect a tear in the corner of his left eye. My day is made.

There is a prison school staffed with teachers who care. But school is scary to people who had trouble with school rules when they were young – and a prison school has lots of rules. There is a prison library. But a library is intimidating to those with limited reading skills. Every shelf is a reminder of their weakness. Prison is no place to show weakness. We are not allowed to receive books through the mail – they could contain drugs, we are told. There is no Internet, and the few computers here are occupied as soon as one is available. Reading must be struggled for in prison.

A group of volunteer literacy tutors from Cowansville, mostly retired teachers, visit the prison chapel two Fridays a month. They belong to the Yamaska Literacy Council, a band of tutors and tutor trainers. They have been operating as an organization for a full thirty years in this small prison-agricultural supply town an hour east of Montreal. These Yamaska volunteers train prisoner tutors and work with students. The chaplain, once a teacher himself, makes coffee and provides space. He steps back and discretely helps out when he can. Books are brought in. Glittering certificates are given out – it is important to mark and celebrate success. Between these visits, it is up to us.

It is a gray, windy Saturday. The prison factory does not need me today. Marven is emotional. "When I get out", he tells me, "I'll be able to read to my grandchildren, you know. I won't have to say, 'I'm busy, go ask your mother'. They'll be shocked". A smile creeps across his lips. Illiteracy is something to be hidden if you are a large, muscle-bound man with responsibilities and pride. The secret gnaws at a man's soul. Historically, the illiteracy rate among senior citizens in Brome Missisquoi County – the half-Anglophone, largely agricultural district where the prison sits – has been very high. For instance, Calamai (1987) estimated the rate to be around two-thirds of that segment of the population. The older you are, the less likely you are to be able to read. My 65-year-old friend is not alone. The Yamaska Literacy Council has its work cut out for it.

We are now under Marven's lucky tree when it starts to rain. Tiny watermarks spread across the open pages of our book like ink blots on a Rorschach test. Indoors, recreation rooms are packed with poker players. We have nowhere to go. Marven shrugs his shoulders. "We can come back tomorrow, right?", he asks. "Unless my shoulder acts up. Boy I'm in pain a lot". He raises his arm to show me where it hurts. The pain is not that bad, really. He is just scared that one day the progress he is making will stop, that suddenly he will not be able to read. Nothing I say will calm his fears. The next day, he might come back. If not, I will bring my novel and read alone under the lucky tree with the gentle breeze as my companion. For an hour I will not be in prison. I will be in the Land of Shadows.

The Yamaska Literacy Council has been coming to Cowansville Institution for a decade. For many years, the Council operated under the aegis of a worldwide literacy program, Laubach Literacy International. It is the world's foremost adult literacy training organization, and has taught over 100 million adults to read and write worldwide. Its beginnings give clues to its success in the prisons. In the 1920s, a young Congregationalist missionary named Dr. Frank C. Laubach found himself sent to the Philippines, specifically, to the island of Mindanao, then as now home to Muslim tribes. Laubach found himself among the Moros, a particularly bellicose tribe whose members lived along or near the water in huts raised on poles. They had an oral language, Maranaw, but no written script (Laubach and Norton, 1990).

Laubach decided to alphabetize their language. Happily, Maranaw is a Polynesian dialect, the simplest language family in the world to alphabetize. A related tongue, Hawaiian, is famous for having only twelve letters. Laubach boiled Maranaw's sounds down to fourteen Roman letters. By trial and error, he discovered the value of using key words to help students identify individual sounds; then, he created a series of charts using a key word and picture for each chart. Illiterate tribesmen were reading within two weeks (ibid).

When the Great Depression hit, Dr. Laubach's church ran out of money. He told the Moros that he had to go home. The tribal chief had another idea: "I'll make everybody who knows how to read teach somebody else", he declared, "*or I'll kill him!*" Oddly, the chief's scheme worked brilliantly. Laubach went home and adopted the system into English, a bird-shaped as the letter B, for example. From the Moro chief's death threat came the Laubach organization's motto: Each One Teach One. The death threat was removed to appeal to a wider audience (ibid). Given Laubach Literacy's rough and tumble beginnings, it was and is ideally suited for prisoners.

The Yamaska Literacy Council was part of a national organization, Laubach Literacy Canada, which did yeoman's work in prisons and in other dark corners of our country. A few years ago, the Harper government, in its infinite wisdom, decided to no longer fund adult literacy programs of any kind. Their rationale: if a person has not learned to read by the time they are eighteen, tough cookies. It is not the government's job. Laubach Literary Canada folded. The Yamaska Literacy Council was stuck with a funding shortfall, set adrift from their umbrella organization. But they did not disband and they did not forget the prisoners they had worked with for many years.

At the time, I had been volunteering as a tutor here for quite a while. Indeed, in 2004, the locals chose me (unwisely, said some of the prison's staff) to become Canada's only Laubach-accredited tutor training behind bars. I was put through an intensive course, including a good eight hundred pages of printed material to learn cold for a series of exams. Remarkably, I passed. I went on to help train prisoner tutors, alongside the community volunteers. Things are going very well today. We have seven prisoner tutors and upwards of twenty students. We use the various accredited exercise books, dictionaries, and easy readers provided as part of the program. The prison is laid back and very accommodating as a rule to our activities. It helps a lot that the Yamaska Literacy Council crew are pillars of the local community.

There have been hiccups. Operating in a prison environment can be challenging. Transfers and releases mean a high turnover rate of tutors and students. One of our students stabbed another in a dispute over a poker game, away from tutoring activities. Happily, no one was seriously hurt. Some of our volunteers, who are mostly women, were somewhat disturbed by an prisoner tutor with no lack of self-esteem and stopped coming until the man was transferred to another prison. I myself have been at this prison for over ten years at the time of writing – my case involved CSC and police folk. For some years, because of my refusal to accede to some of the demands of my case management team, it was strongly suggested that preventative security officers did not want me to darken the doors of the chapel while the Yamaska Literacy Council volunteers were present.

I tutored alone inside the cellblocks. My reports read that I thought I was a "Tudor" rather than a "tutor". All that is now in the past. After twenty years in prison, they stop pressuring you. After twenty years in medium, if you are not yet in a minimum, you are not going to see freedom, ever, they say. I am now ignored, free to tutor at the chapel.

This medium-security facility is not by any means the most dangerous prison in Canada. Still, volunteers should be commended for their bravery. Some of these retired teachers are pretty tough themselves. One elfin lady referred to as the "literacy princess" is not averse to telling hardened prisoners, myself included, to "screw off" when required. And we obey.

Yamaska Literacy Council volunteers, both in the prison and in the community, focus much of their efforts on training tutors who then go on to teach others, always on a one-to-one basis, as this approach has been proven over time to be the most effective way of imparting literacy skills to adult learners (*Basic Literacy*, 2012). They work quite a bit at the local high school, Massey-Vanier, a few hundred yards from the prison chapel, invisible to us beyond our fences and a tall stand of trees. The Laubach approach is non-confrontational, caring and encouraging, perfectly suited for prisoners who are, as a rule, somewhat resentful of authority. "In a literacy campaign", wrote Dr. Laubach, "we need faith, hope, love – these three; and the greatest of all love. It has no substitutes. When it fails, everything else fails" (Laubach and Kirk, 1990). This sort of sensitivity to adults struggling with their literacy skills is the hallmark of the Laubach approach.

English is not necessarily an easy tongue to learn. Its vowels can be pronounced a total of eighteen different ways. The nonsense word "ghoti" can conceivably be pronounced as *fish* (think of the "gh" in *tough*; the "o" in *women*; the "ti" in *nation*). The *Oxford English Dictionary* spends seven and a half pages defining the word "round", and offers 194 separate ways to use the word "set". An adult learning English has to work at it. To that end, our students are encouraged to write, and some have won awards for their short reviews of specially written, easy-to-read books.

There are several prisoners here with post-secondary educations in English. These are men (and one transgender person) who enjoy imparting their knowledge to prisoners with literacy difficulties or to those from outside Canada struggling with the mysteries of English. Prisoner tutors go through the same twelve-hour training program that literacy trainees complete under the aegis of the Yamaska Literacy Council anywhere else. "It's one of the few productive, positive things you can take with you when you leave these walls", says Domingo Lecompte, a tutor who speaks four languages and works with Latinos.

After that, we all improvise. "The challenge here", says tutor Ed Callery, who attended the University of Florida, "is to use different approaches until you find out how to reach a student. That's the key to success as a tutor". A stroke victim, Ed uses his personal situation as a resource, patiently working alongside students with limited literacy skills.

Robert Sargeant, a University of Western Ontario alum who enjoys working with more advanced students, puts it more succinctly: "Experience trumps assumptions". This statement is also applicable in a general way to this strange bimonthly Yamaska Literacy Council prison phenomenon.

There are other adult literacy programs in prisons and outside prisons too. But overall, adult literacy teaching in Canada has become, in the era of government cutbacks, a decentralized, grassroots entity by necessity. Canada's Frontier College (www.frontiercollege.ca) first taught lumbermen to read in logging camps, working by lamplight in tents. It is now nationwide and is particularly active in Ontario's justice system.

For Francophones, there is a *Fondation québecoise pour l'alpabetisation* (www.fqa.qc.ca), though no French language outside tutors visit Cowansville Institution (Yamaska Literary Council's initiative is very much a local Eastern Townships English community thing). As a lifelong Quebec Anglophone, I can attest to the liberal, open-minded nature of this region's remaining English-speaking peoples. Indeed, when one of our tutors transferred to another jail, he was counselled not to contact the local adult education organization serving the area in which his new institution was located. "They applaud our efforts", one of the Yamaska co-ordinators told me, "but they want no part of prison literacy". Laubach, as far as anyone knows, is the only group to actually accredit and train prisoner tutors to work one-on-one with other prisoners.

Institutional schools in Canada's corrections systems are staffed as a rule by teachers, employed by a local school board, working on contract. They are trained adult education professionals who happen to come to work in a place like this. One prison educator once told me that there is little difference between working in a jail's school and working at the adult education centre in a major town a few miles away. Students there struggle with the same issues as prisoners – histories of substance abuse, learning disabilities, disadvantaged upbringings, even criminal records. Prisoners in jails across Canada serve as teacher's aides.

Interested citizens wishing to get involved in prison literacy, or in any sort of volunteer capacity within the correctional system, should get in touch with their local institution or regional office. Other websites of possible interest include: The Canadian Literacy and Learning Network (www.literacy.ca), ABC Canada (www.abclifeliteracy.ca), and the National Adult Literacy Database (www.nald.ca).

With the first snows, the picnic tables disappear from our prison yard. Ed Callery is in Marven's cellblock. I am not and therefore cannot go to his cell. This past winter, several nights a week, Ed would sit with Marven, usually for about half an hour, and read. Alone. Marven would complete long, laborious writing exercises – short, simple words, longhand in discursive script. He completed his *Laubach Way to Reading* Level I text, meriting a certificate for his accomplishment. "He gets excited reading", Ed observes. "It means he won't give up".

Marven turned 66 this spring. He is not fully literate yet, but he knows all the letters of the alphabet and their sounds. He can recognize many dozens of words by spelling them out, pronouncing each piece of the linguistic puzzle until he can form a whole. And he recognizes many dozens of words on sight, especially those he encountered during his rural youth. Ask him to spell "apple" or "farm" and you will get a rapid response.

April brings clement weather to southern Quebec. The picnic tables return to their places in the jail yard. Easter weekend finds me once again under Marven's tree. He brings along his brand new *Oxford Picture Dictionary*, a present from the Yamaska Literary Council. Together we turn to the pages on human anatomy and go over the basic parts of the human body. Marven insists on writing each word out, laboriously, in pencil, in his notebook, pronouncing each letter, then each completed word. We turn to the section on farms. He recognizes a silo and a hay bale and writes those words out. He chats animatedly about picking apples for his grandpa for fifty cents a day and having to carry the money all the way home to his mom, or else.

We get to the section on fruits and vegetables. Marven points at the lemon, looks at me, smiles, and says, "C-O-L-I-N. Colin!" He is clearly enjoying the act of reading.

REFERENCES

Calamai, Peter (1987) *Broken Words: Why Five Million Canadians Are Illiterate*, Toronto: Southam Newspaper Group.

Laubach, Frank and Elizabeth M. Kirk (1990) *Teacher's Manual for Skill Books*, Syracuse, (NY): Laubach Literacy International.

Laubach, Frank and Karen A. Norton (1990) *One Burning Heart*, Syracuse, (NY): Laubach Literacy International.

Movement for Canadian Literacy (2003) *Strengthening Our Literacy Foundation Is Key To Canada's Future: Recommendations for the House of Commons Standing Committee on Human Resources Development and the Status of Persons With Disabilities*. Retrieved from http://www.literacy.ca/content/uploads/2012/02/strengthapr2003.pdf

Yamaska Literacy Council (no date) *Basic Literacy Tutor Handbook*, Cowansville, (QC).

ABOUT THE AUTHOR

Colin McGregor was born and raised in Montreal. He attended Marianopolis College, obtained a BA in Philosophy from McGill University and a graduate diploma in Public Administration from Carleton University, where he taught writing to first-year undergraduate students. Mr. McGregor worked as a newspaper reporter and editor, and as a lobbyist and government communications officer. He has been in prison since 1991 and is riddled with remorse for the actions that led to his incarceration.

What Is Compassionate Release?
Timothy Muise

Compassionate release is used in critical situations when a prisoner is very seriously or terminally ill and when a home-care, hospice, or hospital setting would be more appropriate to meet the person's medical needs while making that care less of a burden upon the taxpayer and society as a whole.

In 1984, a federal law was passed allowing for the compassionate release of prisoners in the custody of the Federal Bureau of Prisons. This law detailed the requirements for compassionate release, in part, as "the unusual case in which the prisoner's circumstances are so changed, such as by terminal illness, that it would be inequitable to continue the confinement of the prisoner" (New York Times, 2012).

From 1992 through November of 2012, a period in which a population of federal prisoners almost tripled from around 80,000 to 220,000 prisoners, the bureau only released 492 people under this program (New York Times, 2012). In Massachusetts, the current prison population is approximately 11,723 prisoners (Massachusetts Department of Corrections, 2011). In the last three years, the number of prisoners over sixty has grown from 656 in 2009 to 692 in 2010 to 740 in 2011 (Massachusetts Department of Corrections, 2009; 2010; 2011) – the fastest growing age group in prison. The second fastest growing age group is fifty to fifty-nine, which is keeping the pipeline full for more growth of the sick and dying. It is anticipated that this percentage will increase exponentially due to the lack of first-degree life sentence commutations, the increase of harsher sentencing such as Melissa's Bill, and the drastic reduction of second-degree lifer paroles here in the Commonwealth after paroled lifer Dominic Cinelli shot a Woburn police officer in 2012 (Haas, 2012). In short order, Massachusetts will be at a crisis stage with its aging prisoner population, and a real and working compassionate release vehicle, unlike the one underutilized in the federal system, will be the only effective avenue of relief.

According to James Austin and the Urban Institute project, by 2030 one third of all prisoners in the United States will be aged fifty-five or older (American Civil Liberties Union, 2012). In Massachusetts, the Division of Capital Asset Management, in its strategic capital plan for the correction's medical population, confesses that acute care capabilities are very limited and not staffed to the level typical of acute care provided in a hospital setting, and that sub-acute care beds are lacking in meeting the needs. In this strategic plan, the state concludes that the most pressing need is the estimated 635 prisoners suffering from long-term chronic illness requiring sub-acute care, when there are only thirteen current beds available (Massachusetts Division of Capital Asset Management, 2011). A medical release option would help to alleviate this extreme shortcoming in the prison infrastructure.

Capital infrastructure aside, the 2011 Massachusetts state prison budget was a whopping $517,000,000. Prisoner healthcare represents 18.48 percent of that budget, ringing in at an astronomical $95,600,000 (Massachusetts Department of Corrections, 2011). A significant part of that healthcare cost is the result of the aging prisoner demographic and the high cost of such geriatric medical needs. I could not secure the figures on how much it costs for security staff to transport these aging prisoners who no longer pose any threat to the safety of the public to and from various hospitals around the state (there are dozens of such transports each day with at least two guards in attendance and on the payroll), but I can tell you that the employee salary aspect of the total budget weighs in at $352,175,000, a staggering 68 percent of the total cost of running prisons (Massachusetts Department of Corrections, 2011).

If aging prisoners were placed in the care of managed care facilities, there would be an immediate benefit in the loss of security staffing costs and independent contract ambulance costs, as well as the higher cost of this type of hospital care being vastly reduced. Keeping these sick and dying men in prison no longer serves the welfare of society, with not only unacceptable financial costs, but also with an even more damaging erosion of the social fabric, which only works to promote the core issues behind crime and incarceration. We must stop the dog from chasing its tail.

Only ten states currently do not have some type of medical release program in their prison systems. Most New England states (New Hampshire, Connecticut, Rhode Island, and Vermont) have such measures (O'Shea, 2010). Massachusetts has made multiple attempts over the years to legislate such a program. For instance, in 1993 Bill No. 4169 on compassionate release passed both houses, but was vetoed by Governor Weld in his draconian approach to prison management. Again in 1997 the same thing happened. In the 2012 Massachusetts's legislative session, state senator Patricia Jehlen (D-Somerville) filed Senate Bill No. 1213, which detailed a workable and cost-effective medical release plan. Massachusetts Governor Deval Patrick also filed similar legislation, although more restrictive and exclusionary, so the idea is making some form of headway in the state house as many see that the chickens are coming home to roost sooner than later as far as the geriatric prisoner population is concerned.

It may be argued that an individual can file for a commutation when their health drastically deteriorates and no new legislation is needed. Such unsubstantiated journalism argues that there is such an "out" through the commutation process, but that is not true in reality (Jacoby, 2006). In a 2003 address to the American Bar Association, U. S. Supreme Court Justice Anthony Kennedy noted that pardons have now become infrequent and the pardon process has been "drained of its moral force" (Mauer *et al.*, 2004, p. 29). In the last sixteen years no one has received a commutation for any reason. In addition, from 2004 to 2008, 184 petitions for commutations were filed, only two were granted a hearing, and neither received a commutation in Massachusetts. In effect, the commutation process as a vehicle for a dying person to leave prison is a defunct system that exists only on paper.

In the 2013 legislative session, Senator Jehlen plans on filing a new bill, as No. 1213 died in chamber last session. Massachusetts CURE plans on working closely with Senator Jehlen, as well as with the Coalition for Effective Public Safety, on promoting and supporting this measure. The time is long overdue for compassionate medical release here in the Commonwealth. We must temper justice with mercy, while ensuring that taxpayer dollars are spent on efforts that will enhance public safety, reduce crime and move us ahead as a society.

REFERENCES

American Civil Liberties Union (2012) *At America's Expense: The Mass Incarceration of the Elderly*, New York (NY).

Haas, Gordan (2012) *The Massachusetts Parole Board*. Retrieved from http://www.realcostofprisons.org/writing/haas_2012_stats.pdf.

Jacoby, Jeff (2006) "The fallacy of life in prison", *The Boston Globe* – February 8.

Massachusetts Department of Correction (2011) *Annual Report*.

Massachusetts Department of Correction (2010) *Annual Report*.

Massachusetts Department of Correction (2009) *Annual Report*.

Massachusetts Division of Capital Asset Management (2011) *Corrections Master Plan*. Retrieved from http://www.mass.gov/eopss/docs/eops/publications/the-massachusetts-corrections-master-plan.pdf.

Mauer, Marc, Ryan S. King, and Malcolm C. Young (2004) "The Meaning of 'Life': Long Prison Sentences in Context", *The Sentencing Project*, Washington (D.C.).

New York Times (2012) "What Compassionate Release?" – December 8. Retrieved from http://www.nytimes.com/2012/12/09/opinion/sunday/what-compassionate-release.html?_r=0.

O'Shea, Patrick (2010) "Facts on Medical Release", *2000 NE Journal on Criminal & Civil Confinement.*

ABOUT THE AUTHOR

Timothy J. Muise is a prisoner-rights activist who is serving an 18-to-20 year prison term for a tragic manslaughter conviction. He works to enhance public safety through addressing negative confinement conditions, while also breaking prisoner stereotypes. He can be reached at:

Timothy J. Muise
P. O. Box 1218,
Shirley, MA 01464-1218
USA.

The Zombification of Formerly Incarcerated and Convicted People: Radical Democracy, Insurgent Citizenship, and Reclaiming Humanity
Grace Gámez

INTRODUCTION

"Sometimes human places create inhuman monsters".

– Stephen King,
The Shining.

This article examines the relationship between zombies and formerly incarcerated/convicted people (FICP),[1] while at the same time exploring what it means to be human. I argue that the major characteristics of zombies are similar to those attributed to formerly incarcerated and convicted people. Although zombies are, of course, fantastical creatures, we understand a great deal about their ontology. Contemporary popular culture provides information about zombies that has constructed our consumption of them. Zombies serve as an endless source of material for entertainment. The "beingness" of zombies is revealed through novels, comic books, films and television shows. From these sources we know, for example, that zombies have an insatiable drive to consume flesh. They are also presumed to lack true consciousness and be incapable of reason, empathy or emotion. Zombies signify the shedding of what was once human — former human beings that have been reanimated into a world that no longer wants them. Because they are portrayed as predators, the living body politic has come to believe zombies are to be feared, avoided and despised. Their Otherness, and soullessness, make it possible to kill them with impunity.

With the popularity of television series such as AMC's *The Walking Dead* (2010-present), zombies have become monsters we are all familiar with. In a similar way, with its endless options of crime-related drama and reality TV to choose from, popular culture has educated the American public about the nature of FICP. The news media is remarkably similar in terms of its function. By sensationalizing stories and offering flat, one-dimensional villains these sources offer the public characters that are other than human, neither living nor dead. Thus, it becomes possible for the public to similarly dismiss their humanity. Moreover, laws and policies remain among the most powerful regulatory tools outside of the media. One of the most common descriptive features of zombies is that they are creatures that occupy a position closer to death than life. Likewise, formerly incarcerated and convicted people, because they are dead in the law, reside at the edge of humanity.

Orlando Patterson's work *Slavery and Social Death* (1982), argued that slavery in America was tantamount to 'social death' because, in part, those it held in captivity were torn apart from connectivity with the social world. Recalling this argument, Loïc Wacquant (2005, p. 130) argues that, "mass incarceration also induces the civic death of those it ensnares by extruding them from the social compact, thereby making them *civiliter mortui*". Wacquant continues by saying that this population is outcast from society, first, by the state and, second, by a fearful citizenry. In the remainder of this article, I argue that these tactics of exclusion work together to render FICP illegible as fellow human beings. Wacquant (2005, pp. 130-132) writes that prisoners [which can be extended to FICP] in many cases, are denied access to higher education, social welfare (including Medicaid), public housing and Section 8, and are banned from political participation.

The marker of criminality/deviance attached to these populations serves to purposefully construct FICP as socially and politically disposable. Using the Formerly Incarcerated & Convicted People's Movement (FICPM) as a lens, I explore how FICP, through employing strategies from below, practice a form of insurgent citizenship, reclaiming and rearticulating their own political agency and human dignity. The present piece considers what it means when a population that is written outside of the law organizes and demands rights and inclusion in a polity that they have been outcast from. In other words, if the law can make and unmake people as Colin Dayan (2011) argues in *The Law is a White Dog*, is the reverse also possible? Can people "unmake" the law?

Before entering into this discussion, I will present a brief survey of the literature on prison and welfare reform, demonstrating that welfare reform acts in symbiotic relationship to mass incarceration to criminalize and disappear, at a disproportionate rate, those who have historically been deemed illegitimate by the state, specifically black and brown people. Indeed, one of the primary arguments of this article, that law wields the power to zombify people, is embedded in issues of racial (in)justice.

Brief Historical Background of the Modern Prison System

> "You hear these white people talk about they've pulled themselves up by
> their own bootstraps. Well they took our boots, no less our straps, and then
> after they made us a citizen, honey what did they turn around and do? They
> passed black codes in order to take from us all the benefits of citizenship".
> – "Queen Mother" Audley Moore (1978) in *Freedom Dreams*.

According to Fields (1982), race in America is a by-product of the interface
between slavery and democracy. Race became the primary marker of control
after slavery was abolished. The historical connections between racism,
criminalization, and our modern penal system are important components
of the trajectory of the making and maintenance of the Prison Industrial
Complex (PIC). The 13th Amendment of the United States Constitution
reads, "Neither slavery nor involuntary servitude, except as a punishment
for crime whereof the party shall have been duly convicted, shall exist
within the United States, or any place subject to their jurisdiction". The
caveat, "except as punishment for crime whereof the party shall have been
duly convicted", opened the door to create laws of which only black people
could be found guilty.

As Dayan (2012) notes, the 13th Amendment provides us with the link
between slavery and prisons and its racialized order. Angela Davis (2003,
p. 28) explains this connection in *Are Prisons Obsolete?* Davis writes:

> After the abolition of slavery, former slave states passed new legislation
> revising Slave Codes in order to regulate the behavior of free blacks in
> ways similar to those that had existed during slavery. The new Black Codes
> proscribed a range of actions, such as vagrancy, absence of work[…]insulting
> gestures or acts [as criminal] only when the person charged was black.

The result was that a newly freed black person could be legally re-enslaved
and sold under the new convict leasing program.

The convict leasing program began in 1866, and the last state to terminate
the program was Alabama in 1928 (Mancini, 1996). As part of the program,
convicts were sold to private parties, such as railroad companies, coalmines
and former plantation owners to work under inhospitable conditions,
violence, and extreme brutality (Mancini, 1996). According to Mancini
(1978, p. 339) in *Race, Economics and the Abandonment of Convict Leasing*:

Convict leasing[…]is best understood[…]as part of the elaborate social
system of racial subordination which had previously been assured by the
practice of slavery[…]the lease system was a component of that larger
web of law and custom which[…]insured the[…]racial hierarchy[…]the
brutality of convict leasing fits clearly into a more comprehensive pattern
of intimidation and violence, and it can be seen as an intrinsic part of that
system rather than an aberration.

Convict leasing is an example of how racial subordination is part of the
fabric of U.S. notions of citizenship and democracy. Additionally, convict
leasing is a part of the history of the penal system, just as racial subordination
is part of that same history. In the convict leasing system, we have proof that
racism was part of the foundation that prison systems were built upon, the
vestiges of which are still seen and felt today.[2] Convict leasing proved to be
lucrative in rebuilding after the Civil War; there was an obvious benefit in
criminalizing the movements of black people who comprised the majority
of those affected by the program.

Prior to emancipation, black people were not sentenced to hard labour or
imprisonment because this would not alter the circumstances in which they
lived (Davis, 2003). Because of this, the majority of people incarcerated
were white before emancipation. For example, Mary Ellen Curtin (2000,
p. 33) writes, "the fast-rising number of Black prisoners in the 1870s and
1880s and the near absence of incarcerated whites illustrate the racial
impact of an increasingly repressive legal system". Furthermore, according
to a study cited by Angela Davis (2003, p. 29):

Before the four hundred thousand black slaves in that state [of Alabama]
were set free, ninety-nine percent of prisoners in Alabama's penitentiaries
were white [as a result of] the shifts provoked by the institution of the
Black Codes, within a short period of time, the overwhelming majority of
Alabama's convicts were black.

This racial disparity remains true as black men and women comprise a significant
percentage of those incarcerated in U.S. prisons (Prison Activist Resource Center:
Fact Sheets).[3] Although convict leasing was eventually terminated, it conditioned
the possibility of Jim Crow laws, which served to further disenfranchise and
legally unmake black and other communities of colour.

Jim Crow laws began in 1875 during the Reconstruction era to prevent
racial integration and participation in public spheres (Sandoval-Strausz,

2005). One of the purposes of Jim Crow laws was to dissuade black people and other people of colour from participating in the polity as rights-bearing citizens of the United States. The other function of the Jim Crow regime was to rework and re-entrench racial distinctions between slaves and free folk, as well as to enforce "a rigid caste separation" (Wacquant, 2005, p. 127). Jim Crow laws overlapped with the convict leasing program, but continued beyond the duration of convict leasing. They remained in place until 1965. These laws took the form of "poll taxes, literacy tests, and other discriminatory regulations to keep African Americans away from voting booths. They [the people enforcing Jim Crow laws] also relied on terrorism and fraud to frighten black citizens who tried to exercise their rights" (Tenney, 2008, p. 1).

This system segregated black people from white people in most public settings. Jim Crow laws forced people of colour to use separate drinking fountains, eat in separate restaurants, live in separate neighbourhoods, and attend separate schools. Laws prohibited intermarrying as well. The reality was that the aforementioned spaces were not only separate but unequal as well (Tenney, 2008; Perman, 2001; Feldman, 2004; Kousser, 1974). According to Michelle Alexander (2010, p. 34) in *The New Jim Crow: Mass Incarceration in the Era of Colorblindness*, "Segregation laws were proposed as a part of a deliberate effort to drive a wedge between poor whites and African Americans". This racial division was meant to inculcate a sense of superiority over black folks for whites, which would prevent alliances aimed at dismantling the power structure (Alexander, 2010). The effect of Jim Crow laws on black – and other communities of colour that they impacted – was reduced, or negligible, access to life-giving human rights such as employment opportunities, quality education, health care, and housing. Furthermore as Cacho (2012, p. 40) writes, "[Jim Crow] criminalized and reified marginalized identities and statuses. Being 'coloured' was a status that formed the basis for exclusionary, discriminatory, and regulatory laws".

The Jim Crow Era ended with the passage of the Civil Rights Act of 1964 and the Voting Rights Act of 1965 (Alexander, 2010). With the close of the Jim Crow era, a familiar rhetoric entered into national discourse once again. It was the same rhetoric deployed after emancipation that made the convict leasing program possible, as well as Jim Crow: a rhetoric of discipline, security and order, which once again targeted black people, other people of colour, and poor people for state surveillance and control.

From the literature cited above we can deduce that slavery, Black Codes, convict leasing, and Jim Crow were state-sanctioned interventions whose intention and result was to exert legal and extra-legal control over a group of people for capital gain. The above-cited literature also charts the history of negative personhood and demonstrates a continuum along which slavery, confinement, and other forms of state surveillance are plotted, as well as a site where whiteness, as Cacho (2012) argues, is decriminalized. The legal mechanisms noted in this section also illustrate that notions of personhood are bound up in how people are understood under the rubric of the 'the right to have rights'. As organizing logics, the three pillars of white supremacy, defined by Smith (2006) as slavery/capitalism, genocide/colonialism, and orientalism/war, along with heteropatriarchy, informed notions of who was considered fully human in the United States.

This section frames the remainder of the literature review as it connects these historical antecedents to modern institutional and ideological structures of the U.S. justice system, which continues to (re)produce systematized inequality and rationalize state-facilitated violence (Rodrìguez, 2006; Escobar, 2010; James, 2007; Sexton, 2010). The scholarship that follows demonstrates how the justice system, and its arm, social welfare, operate as a racialized apparatus of social control to manage marginal populations (Wacquant, 2001; Wacquant 2009; Davis, 2003; Davis 2005; Rodrìguez, 2006; Escobar, 2009; Camp, 2009; Alexander, 2010).

MANAGING SOCIAL MARGINALITY: EXAMINING THE RELATIONSHIP BETWEEN INCARCERATION AND SOCIAL WELFARE REFORM

"In the animal kingdom, the rule is, eat or be eaten; in the human kingdom, define or be defined".

– Thomas Szasz,
The Second Sin.

The criminal justice system has demonstrated itself time and again to be anti-black and anti-poor, but more importantly, as the racial impact of policies such as "Stop and Frisk" have come under public scrutiny, it has become apparent that it is levied as a weapon of social control for specific demographics. However, the work of Ruth Wilson Gilmore (1999, p. 174), suggests the above analysis falls short in fully accounting for "how prison achieved such a central place in structuring the state and shaping the landscape" (also see Camp, 2013).

In order to tease out this relationship, Gilmore (1999; 2002; 2007) focuses on the period of the late 1960s and early 1970s. During this time period, the U.S. was experiencing major shifts both socially and economically. This was a time of a number of radical, multi-racial movements for social justice and civil unrest in the country. Social crisis intensified in the early 1970s, and was accompanied by an "economic panic" over the falling rate of profit and the expansion of the social wage to previously excluded groups (Prashad, 2005; Camp, 2013). This led to a reconceptualization of the labour market, which "expelled from the workforce modestly educated people in the prime of their life who once might have gained their wages making and moving things" (Gilmore, 1999, p. 182). This added to the social emergency.

The task of state actors was to find a way out of both crises. By building prisons they were able to put back to work surpluses of finance capital, land, labour, and warehouse people that were economically marginalized and/or politically dangerous (Gilmore, 2007). In this way, the "prison fix" emerged as a "geographic solution to socio-economic problems organized by the state, which is also in the process of restructuring" (Gilmore, 1999, p. 174). Importantly, what Gilmore (1999; 2002; 2007) and others observed was that the state remade itself by building prisons (also see Garland, 2001; Wacquant, 2009; Camp, 2013). In other words, "The United States: Prison Nation" did not evolve as such because of "a mechanical response to economic changes so much as an *exercise in state crafting* aimed at producing – and then adapting to – these very changes[...It was] a *specifically political project* aimed at remaking not only the market but also and above all, the state itself" (Wacquant, 2009, p. 103, original emphasis).

This explanation helps make sense of the contradictions found in mainstream accounts of why we have so many people in prison. Namely, that crime and, in particular, the economy of illicit drugs, has steadily increased over time. However, crime and drug use has in fact gone down steadily since the U.S. began building prisons in earnest in the 1980s (Gilmore, 2007). Despite this reality the economy of investing in, building and maintaining prisons is a booming industry. The reality does not match up with justice related responses. We find then that mass incarceration is not related to crime, but rather, fueled by political manoeuvrings to respond to state crises. As demonstrated in the previous section, the new state that evolved was "not unexpected nor without roots" (in genocide, slavery, colonialism, and movement suppression) as Gilmore (1999, p. 178) reminds us. Rather, the United States' "modus operandi for solving crises has been the relentless identification, coercive control and violent elimination of foreign and domestic enemies" (ibid).

We see then that legislation based on racialized security ideologies garnered support for policy that manages social marginality through criminalization. This project was made possible by increasing the amount of money funneled into the criminal justice system that included passing sentencing reforms such as mandatory minimums and three strikes legislation, as well as militarizing law enforcement operations (Gilmore, 2007; Waquant, 2009; Meiners, 2011). This was accompanied by a retreat from social welfare programs, which had a profound effect on women and in particular women of colour.

Frances Fox Piven and Richard Cloward argue in *Regulating the Poor* (1993, p. xvii), "relief programs are initiated to deal with dislocations in the work system that lead to mass disorder and are then retained (in an altered form) to enforce work". The dynamic described is one of expansion and contraction of public aid in order to regulate and pacify the poor. This relationship evolved into a criminalization of the poor, beginning most dramatically in the mid-1990s when the net of punishment expanded. With the passage of the 1996 Personal Responsibility and Work Opportunities Reconciliation Act (PRWORA), social welfare underwent dramatic cut-backs and the language surrounding the right to public aid transformed into pathologizing the poor as deviant. According to Linda Burnham (2001, p. 39), "The stated intent of welfare reform was at least twofold: to reduce the welfare rolls and to move women toward economic self-sufficiency". The state has been successful on the first objective but has failed on the second. Burnham writes that women have in fact fared poorly in becoming financially established; many are able to secure only low-paying jobs that do not offer long-term stability or "lift their families above the poverty line...they work hard and remain poor" (ibid).

Indeed the feminization of poverty has been well documented as well as the ways in which poverty constructs the lives of children that it affects. In *Lives on the Edge: Single Mothers and their Children in the 'Other' America,* Valerie Polakow (1993) offers harrowing narratives of mothers and their children who occupy 'otherized' spaces, who they themselves become 'other', precisely because of their poverty. Polakow adds to the argument that poverty is socially produced, reproduced and contributes to the discussion of the racialization of welfare, which has morphed into a criminalization of the poor.

While *most* laws and policies appear to be race neutral in the way they are written, their impact is not. Welfare reform has had its greatest impact on families of colour because like most social ills, poverty is racialized and gendered. This is evidenced in the U.S. Department of Health and Human Services report (2010) The data shows that 31.8 percent of Temporary Assistance Needy Families (TANF) recipients were white, while 61.9 percent were black and Latino.[4] This statistic demonstrates that the burden of reform is being shouldered by families of colour; indeed, the racialization of welfare has made the very word 'welfare' synonymous with 'urban' black and Latina single mothers. This connection has lead to welfare recipients being held in contempt and disregard by the American public. In *Welfare Racism*, Neubeck and Cazenave (2001, p. 4) write that surveys reveal that "[w]hen welfare recipients are seen as being mostly white they are likely to be thought of with compassion; when they are seen as being mostly black they are viewed with contempt". This racialization of welfare has turned into a criminalization of the poor.

The expansion of the regulation and punishing of the poor as seen in the disaster of the welfare apparatus interfaces with the carceral network. In *Punishing the Poor*, Loïc Wacquant (2009, p. xvi) outlines three factions that intersect with what he argues is a new class structure that itself is structured by neoliberal deregulation. He describes the relationship thusly:

> [First] incarceration serves to physically neutralize and warehouse the supernumerary fractions of the working class and in particular the dispossessed members of stigmatized groups ... [next] the rolling out of police, judicial, and correctional net of the state fulfills the function... of imposing the discipline of desocialized wage work among the established fractions of the proletariat and the declining and insecure strata of the middle class... Lastly...the penal institution serves the symbolic mission of reaffirming the authority of the state and ... political elites to emphasize and enforce the sacred border between commendable citizens and deviant categories, the 'deserving' and 'underserving' poor.

In other words, incarceration is the net that captures those populations that are irrelevant to, have failed at, or who have been rejected from the capitalist order. These dispossessed groups, who are unable to contribute to the accumulation of capital, are deemed not just *financially* unproductive members of society, but *morally* undeserving as well. These are the people who Wacquant argues populate North America's prison system. They are also the same populations who have historically been set up for disparate surveillance and control.

Wacquant asserts that the economy of punishment is structured by both material and symbolic power axes. Analyzing punishment from these two perspectives broadens and complicates our understanding of the penal machine as each communicates certain norms. The materialist perspective traces the relationship between "the penal system and the system of production, while the symbolic outlook is attentive to the capacity that the state has to trace salient social demarcations and produce social reality[...]" (ibid). Though these power structures have typically been studied separately, Wacquant goes on to say that the system of corrections and related policies operates materially and symbolically and in a simultaneous fashion. As such, they should be considered jointly.

In other words, penal institutions and policies communicate standards, while shaping subjectivities (ibid). The workfare and prisonfare systems, as Wacquant calls them, operate on similar logics and have coevolved. Therefore, by looking at the welfare system and its relationship to the prison system, we gain new insight into some of the reasons driving North American prison growth. The management of social marginality through welfare or prison craft is neither a project of the left nor the right; rather, it is a neoliberal endeavour (ibid). Neoliberalism emphasizes deregulation and a severe reduction of state social responsibility, both of which are seen in the evolution of the welfare system.

The *caricature* of the despised welfare queen remains embedded in the American psyche, influencing policy decisions and swaying voters. Although it was a Republican president who sparked welfare benefit cutbacks, it was Democrat Bill Clinton who campaigned on a promise "to end welfare as we know it" (Zucchino, 1997, p. 14). Polakow (1997, p. 247) argues that this promotion of poverty as a personal behavioral condition diverts public attention from what the roots of poverty are – a "diminishing public economy...[and] the histories of class, race and gender discrimination[...]". The discourse and framing of poverty, single mothers and welfare produced a bipartisan policy decision that would have far reaching consequences.

In 1996, President Clinton signed into law the welfare reform act, officially named the Personal Responsibility and Work Opportunity Reconciliation Act (PRWORA). PRWORA indeed ended welfare as it had been known, welfare transferred from a federally managed, to a state managed obligation: it ended the "sixty year old federal cash assistance program, Aid to Families with Dependent Children (AFDC) [and replaced it] with Temporary Assistance to Needy Families (TANF) [which are] block grants to states governed under a new set of time-limits and restrictions" (Marchevsky and Theoharis, 2000, p. 235). The new act set restrictions on who was eligible to receive aid; it banned teenage mothers, newborn babies, people convicted of certain felonies, and *legal* immigrants (Marchevsky and Theoharis, 2000, my emphasis).

The new welfare program became a temporary assistance plan for those deemed deserving, and as its name suggests, focused on getting recipients to take personal responsibility for their poverty – moving them off the rolls and into the workforce. It is within these dynamics that Waquant (2009) argues neoliberalism is the driving force behind the shift from social welfare to penal management of poverty. Although the United States witnessed a rise in the prison population under the Reagan administration (320,000 prisoners to 608,000) the largest increase was seen in the Clinton presidency (851,000 to 1,316,000) (Wacquant, 2009, p. 302). Again because this is a neoliberal project, politicians Right and Left find value/profit in it though the conditions described in the state management of social marginality are not free of historical implications as the working poor and prison population are institutionally and racially stratified (Peck and Theodore, 2000; 2001; 2008).

ON BEING HUMAN: THE ZOMBIFICATION OF FICP

"Fear of being devoured by the walking dead is one thing; fear of being contaminated is another entirely".
    – In *Zombies are Us: Essays on the Humanity of the Walking Dead*

The technologies of power and oppression described in this and the previous section worked to structure social relations along racial axes. Relatedly, the spaces inhabited by people of colour became equally written as being outside of the law and communities of colour became spaces of state violence and oppression. Criminality and social deviance became, and have remained, unarticulated racial signifiers, and prisons/prisoners are constitutive parts of this new social order. Criminality, or rather the production of it, is not unique. Rather, we see from tracing the historical arc that it is a method that has been employed, again, over time, in the (re) making of the United States.

This relationship echoes Michel Foucault's (2003) notion of racism. Foucault suggests that the law functions to reinstate the state and racism functions as a mode of regulatory control. Briefly, he elaborates two logics of biopower: making live and letting die. In reference to the first part of biopower, knowledge and power around institutions (medical, welfare) are gathered to optimize life, thus making segments of the population flourish. Alternately, racism intervenes as a mechanism of the state that creates conditions to "let die" a particular segment of the population, to render them disposable; racialized policing functions as a technology that reinscribes the state (Foucault, 2003). The marker of criminality/deviance previously discussed purposefully constructs incarcerated/formerly incarcerated and convicted people as socially and politically disposable.

In *The Law is a White Dog*, Colin Dayan (2011) argues that people convicted of felonies are regarded as irrelevant to the social order and therefore disposable. As a result of their extraneous position, they live on the fringes of civil society and are forced to take on new ways of being. Dayan argues that their altered state forces the public to consider what it means to exist within the law. She writes that "it is through law that persons[…]gain or lose definition, become victims of prejudice or inheritors of privilege" and once one is written outside of the law their claims for inclusion in the polity become inconsequential to the rest of society (ibid, p. xi). The book seeks to examine how the law upholds philosophies of personhood by examining historical "sites of incapacitation" such as slavery, torture, solitary confinement and preventative detention. Dayan demonstrates that as a society, to reference Avery Gordon (2008), we are haunted by our collective past. Our dependence on the corrections system (i.e. incarceration, community supervision, etc.) means a reliance on a structure that is predicated upon on social/civil disappearance, as well as a history of enslavement to, of all ironies, ensure justice is served. These technologies of domination are, as stated in the introduction of this article, rooted in our laws and policies.

Dayan (2011) traces the rituals of alienation that result from inhabiting the zombie state of being a convicted felon. She writes that this population is "banished from the community, shorn of personality, condemned to degradation[…]The person convicted of felony is alive in fact but dead in law" (ibid, p. 4). Dayan charts this practice of dehumanization back to 1799, when the civil death statute was changed from "shall be deemed dead to all intents and purposes in the law" to read, "thereafter be deemed civilly dead" (ibid, p. 5). This meant that a person convicted of a felony was "[d]ispossessed of all of the benefits of the law, the convict was doomed *in his person* to perpetual incapacitation" (ibid). Living in a state of civil death is in fact what defines the zombie status of FICP. It is a life of disenfranchisement, instability, and precarity, and it is upheld by the law so that punishment extends beyond any sentence of imprisonment or community corrections — it is in reality everlasting.

In a similar way, Cacho (2012, p. 60) writes that the "'value of life' is measured by and made intelligible through the criminal justice system [whereby victims and offenders] are assigned value and valueless-ness not only in relation to one another, but also in relation to already not-valued others". One of the basic arguments of the book is that we are defined by the constitutive "other", where status is reinforced only by what is excluded. Thus, Cacho asserts that when we begin by focusing on social death, from the perspective of those whose voices and experiences are most frequently dismissed and held in contempt, we are better able to analyze whom social rejection actually benefits and harms. Taking up the perspective and struggle of those living in a zombified state — alive, yet civilly dead — may seem like a hopeless cause. However, Cacho rightly argues that "empowerment is not contingent on taking power or securing small victories. Empowerment comes from deciding that the outcome of the struggle doesn't matter as much as the decision to struggle" (ibid, p. 32). She terms this "unthinkable politics", which is a politics that acknowledges the battle may not elicit change. She argues that it is not the same as hopelessness, but rather opening the door to dream different dreams of what makes living life valuable (ibid, pp. 32-33).

The question that remains is how is this leap from death to life made? Dayan (2011) introduces a theoretical remedy for state sanctioned dispossession, a repossession if you will. She relies on the story of Apollonius of Tyana to describe what the crossing over from death to life might entail. The story tells of a young boy bitten by a rabid dog. To heal the boy, Apollonius seeks out the dog responsible and, instead of casting the dog out or killing it, he heals the dog and has "the dog lick the bite, so that the boy's wounder should also be his healer" (ibid, p. 38). The dog, not just the boy, is redeemed. This, then, brings us back to the central question of this article. Using the metaphor of Apollonius, the dog is the law and the question is this: Can the bite that once transformed the living into the dead be used as a remedy? Can the law be manipulated and rearticulated in order to reverse a zombie state? Further, can the mere practicing of "unthinkable politics", making the decision to struggle not, based on whether you will win or not but because you see your worth, be enough to reignite one's humanity?

The FICPM complicates the analysis of those who are selected for life or vulnerability to death and offers an example of what reclaiming humanity, according to Dayan (2011) and Cacho (2012), might look like. The following section of this paper constructs the FICPM as a struggle from below and beyond state power and discusses it as a practice of radical democracy and citizenship, as well as a way to reverse a zombified state.

THE FORMERLY INCARCERATED & CONVICTED PEOPLE'S MOVEMENT

> "[S]tateless people could see...that the abstract nakedness of being nothing but human was their greatest danger...it seems that a man who is nothing but a man has lost the very qualities which make it possible for other people to treat him as a fellow-man. The loss of...political status became identical with expulsion from humanity altogether."
>
> – Hannah Arendt

> "These people don't take nothing from you, as a formerly convicted person, unless it's important...if voting is not important why did they take it?"
>
> – Wayne Jacobs,
> *X-Offenders for Community.*

EMPOWERMENT

On March 7, 2011, fifty formerly incarcerated and convicted activists from across the United States gathered in Alabama to engage in conversations about the need to organize collectively and collaboratively for civil, social, and human rights for incarcerated, formerly incarcerated, and convicted people (Reilly, 2011; Law, 2011). The result of that meeting was the creation of the FICPM, the vision of which was "The fight for the full restoration of our civil and human rights" (Reilly, 2011). The second convening of the FICPM was held on November 2, 2011, in South Central Los Angeles at the Watts Labor Action Center. Over three hundred people attended, and sessions covered topics including Juvenile Justice, Voting Rights, Impact of Mass Incarceration on Families & Communities, and Employment Rights.

As a convicted person myself, it was moving to be in attendance at this conference, partly because it was the first time that I felt a spark of hope and the first time that I made the connection of living a life in a wavering zone between the world of the living and the world of the dead with how rights, or the lack thereof, mediated the two worlds. At the conference, I wrote down a question that on a theoretical level addressed living on the edge of being human and its connection to losing rights.[5] It was this: What does it mean when a critical mass of formerly incarcerated and convicted people organizes to demand rights and inclusion in a polity that they have been outcast from? Does the arc of potentiality (that what can be, can also not be) also apply to the law? In other words, if law can make and unmake people, as argued by Collin Dayan (2011), is the reverse also possible? Can people "unmake" the law? Can a zombie become human again?

Incarcerated, formerly incarcerated, and convicted people are deprived a range of rights that are common in a democracy. Some of these include freedom of movement, access to social welfare, access to education, access to work or financial opportunity, and juridical rights including voting or serving as jurors. How do we conceptualize this population who exist socially but do not and cannot be related to other citizens precisely because of these fundamental markers of inaccessibility?

Margaret Somers (2010), drawing on the work of T.H. Marshall, argues that political membership in a society consists of social and juridical rights. The former includes "the right to social inclusion in civil society [meaning] the right to recognition by others as a moral equal treated by the same standards and values and due the same level of respect and dignity [and] the second, civil-juridical rights, are summed up in Marshallian terms as civil, political, and social rights", social and juridical rights also include human rights (ibid, p. 6).

These rights of membership and inclusion are components of citizenship. However, FICP are divested of political and social voice and therefore become unrecognizable as fellow humans much less as citizens. As such, they are easily subjected to oppression without objection. The following example from the FICPM conference demonstrates how the lack of rights makes inhuman conditions possible. During the session on "Impact of Incarceration on Family", James Adams (2011) from North Carolina and organizer for *All of Us or None* spoke about the issue of disenfranchisement and the impact it has had on his family. He said:

> Many of us recognize that our prison sentence never ends as long as the
> discrimination against us continues. Even our children are denied access to

services. My daughter has Down's Syndrome, when she was four we applied for a scholarship to cover medical expenses and we were denied because I have a felony conviction and spent time in prison. We're organizing because we're not taking just what you [sic] will give us. [...] We have reached the point now that we demand to be treated right (FICPM, personal recording).

We see from this example that the negation of social rights makes possible a system that punishes families of FICP. Indeed, this is because the system does not recognize them, and by extension their families, as human. The trauma illustrated above is only possible when one has been denied the "right to have rights".

According to Agamben (1998) the modern nation-state is founded upon that which it excludes. However, human rights have been long conceived as inalienable rights, regardless of lack of civil-juridical rights. Agamben (2000), referencing Hannah Arendt (1968) in *Imperialism*, discusses this paradox. He writes:

The conception of human rights based on the supposed existence of a human being as such...proves untenable as soon as those who profess it find themselves confronted for the first time with people who have really lost every quality and every specific relation except for the pure fact of being human. In the system of the nation-state, so-called sacred and inalienable human rights are revealed to be without any protection precisely when it is no longer possible to conceive of them as rights of the citizens of a state. (Agamben, 2000, pp. 18-19)

Agamben argues that human rights signify naked life in the juridical order of the nation-state. Without possessing those rights conferred upon citizens, one is reduced to a state of inhuman condition or bare life. Historically, civil death led to actual death since the *homo sacer*, or cursed one, could be killed with impunity. Although FICP experience civil and social death they are not what Agamben would define as *homo sacer* – a person who is *fully* denationalized and unprotected by the law.

Fear causes us to misrecognize ourselves in those who are cast as the "other". Similarly, Stratton (2011) argues that what is most frightening about zombies is the fate of existing in an interstitial state of being between life and death. In the same way people fear the outsider status of FICP—they too are the walking dead. Anthony Downey (2009, p. 109) writes:

Lives lived on the margins of social, political, cultural, economic and geographical borders are lives half lived. Denied access to legal, economic and political redress, these lives exist in a limbo-like state that is largely preoccupied with acquiring and sustaining the essentials of life...they have been outlawed...placed beyond recourse to law and yet still in precarious relationship to law itself.

FICP live at the liminal edge of bare life, excluded from rights and characterized as threats to the living – they live a life exposed to vulnerability and death. For FICP, this space of exception, where the exception becomes norm, extends beyond the physical space of the camp or in this case prison. Because it is their person that remains outside of the law, FICP inhabit a state of indistinction. Though bodily free (not incarcerated), as previously discussed, FICP are unable to access life-giving resources such as welfare benefits, education, and juridical rights. As a consequence, their quality of life is severely diminished. FICP are perpetually suspended in between the space of existence and non-existence, disenfranchised politically, socially, and economically, unable to access many basic human rights and most civil rights, but still implicated in the *bios*[6] – they are zombified.

I argue, however, that FICP are not *trapped* in this zone of indistinction. Those involved in this movement know that without using their voices and collective power to demand rights currently denied to them, a just life is untenable; this is something that is recognized and it is what animates the movement. Therefore they are agents of change in their own right. By enacting "unthinkable politics" they write themselves back into the ledger of humanity.

Practicing Radical Democracy

"All of our issues are all of our issues".

– Tina Reynolds,
WORTH.

In *Hegemony and Socialist Strategy: Towards a Radical Democratic Politics,* Laclau and Mouffe (1985) argue that movements agitating for social and political change must also incorporate a strategy that confronts neoliberal concepts of democracy. The objective is to augment the definition of democracy to include difference, as well as the traditional notions that many connect to democracy, such as freedom and equality. They argue that liberal democracy, instead of building consensus among a diverse populace, suppresses opinions, races, classes and genders that differ from its hegemony. Because difference is a given in society, radical democracy embraces dissent and posits that democracy is dependent upon it. Foregrounding the assumption that oppressive power relations are constantly at play in society, Laclau and Mouffe contend that these hierarchies of power and oppression should be not only be made legible and visible but also contested and altered.

Rasmussen and Brown (2002, p. 175) write that the purpose of radical democratic theory is to "generate an anti-essentialist politics that continually attempts to redefine itself in order to resist the exclusion of individuals and groups in the formation of the social order". I am using radical democratic theory as a tool to interrogate dissent as a practice of democracy and insurgent citizenship in the FICPM.

Although it is state specific, general conditions of parole/probation expressly prohibit parolees/probationers from fraternizing with anyone who has previously been convicted of a crime. Despite this, the people who are organizing and developing platforms in order to demand social and civil-juridical rights from the state are formerly incarcerated and convicted people, some of which are still currently under correctional supervision. In other words, in some instances the organizers, many of the activists, and those in attendance at the FICPM were deliberately breaking the conditions of their probation or parole. For example, a gentleman during the session on voting stood up to ask a question about the federal election system. He said, "My name is Robert, just finished doing thirty-one years in the Federal system, straight, been home five days. On paper my parole lasts until 2069, I will be 119 years old if I live that long" (FICMP, personal recording, 2011). By attending the conference, Robert was most likely in direct violation of the conditions of his release and this infraction could send him right back to prison.

We must ask ourselves why Robert felt that this conference was critical, so much so that he risked at the least a violation on his record and reduction of privileges, and at the most extreme end of the spectrum, re-incarceration. Robert was not the only one; there were over three hundred people in attendance, most of them FICP. Since FICP are in many senses already written outside of the law, it means that in certain cases they may have to break the law or be irresponsible, to challenge the – "commonsense" – of the law in order to, as Laclau and Mouffe (1985) argue, alter it. One is ineligible to vote in most states within the United States while still under supervision of the corrections system. In the case of Robert, it means that he is permanently disenfranchised. I argue that by attending this event, Robert was acting as a political subject and enacting his citizenship (Walters, 2008). He claimed rights that he is technically denied.

The FICPM resides in opposition to the current power bloc. Power, as Rasmussen and Brown (2002) state, operates on many levels, and dictates what can be read as political versus illegal. Because of this response, activities that resist this order must be diverse. Everyday forms of resistance can be read as political acts (Laclau, 1990). For some people, voting may not be possible, at least not immediately. This was not a fact that was lost on activists present at the FICPM. Rosana Cruz of New Orleans, *Voices of the EX-Offender* (VOTE) said:

> We have to be creative about people who don't have the right to vote, people who are currently incarcerated, including undocumented folks [...] what are the other strategies? Let's think about using our economic power to vote, and using boycotts and other systems for civic engagement. Just because you don't vote doesn't mean that you can't go to a city council meeting, it doesn't mean you don't pay taxes, it doesn't mean you aren't civically engaged. So we have to expand the concept of civic engagement beyond voting (FICPM, personal recording, 2011).

Reimagining civic engagement or rethinking what constitutes an act of citizenship within this movement is part of a larger discussion on how rights speak to one's humanity. For this population, they have experienced firsthand the tenuous nature of humanity in the eyes of the state. They *feel* the connection between social and civil-juridical rights and their humanity in their very being. In a reflection on the FICPM, a formerly incarcerated woman "Pilar"[7] said:

> For a long time I have felt less than human, I have questioned whether or not the system has somehow or another rendered me "other" than human. It isn't just the tactics of dehumanization deployed by corrections officers, parole or probation officers, it is everything that comes with being an incarcerated/formerly incarcerated or convicted person – it is being exempted from civil and social life. (Tenacious, 2011, p. 33)

By fighting for the bundle of rights as outlined by T.H. Marshall and Margaret Somers (2008), people in this movement are working to rehumanize themselves and promote democracy to humanize the millions of people in the United States impacted by the prison industrial complex.

INSURGENT CITIZENSHIP

> It is time for us to become the people we have been waiting for. We have the right to ask and answer our own questions and today is the time and place to begin some of that asking and answering. We believe that imprisonment or conviction on a felony charge should not result in a lifelong violation of our basic rights as human beings either while we are on probation, in prison or as we make the transition from prison back into our communities.
>
> – FICPM *Vision Statement.*

In the chapter "Theorizing Acts of Citizenship", Engin Isin (2008, p. 17) evaluates the web of rights and responsibilities entangled in current debates on citizenship by centering acts of citizenship as his object of investigation. By doing so, he argues that he is making a deliberate shift away from critical studies on citizenship, which focuses on "how [citizenship] status becomes contested by investigating practices through which claims are articulated and subjectivities are formed". Though acts and practices are not mutually exclusive, Isin marks a difference between the two. He writes that enacting citizenship outside of formal status requires a break from previous modes of thought and conduct, which are largely based on order and practice. This framework provides a rupturing space to interrogate methods employed from "below" – the new subjects making themselves by challenging dominate orders and clusterings as in the FICPM.

Lacan (1991) argues that acts are imbued with meaning beyond the action itself. Similarly, Arendt (1968, p. 27) posits that acts set in motion and engage in the creation of movements that are "unexpected, unpredictable and unknown". Engaging in acts thus creates agency. As previously discussed, the FICPM was created from the ground up, built by formerly incarcerated, convicted people and allies in response to political and social disenfranchisement. The act is the movement constructed to secure human and civil rights for this population; what roots actors then is not only the content of the act, but also the embodiment of the sense of the act.

Isin (2008, p. 38) argues that without investigating acts it is impossible to theorize citizenship as it arises through them. He offers three principles to summarize his approach to theorizing acts of citizenship. The first principle is to interpret acts "through their grounds and consequences, which includes subjects becoming activist citizens through scenes created". Here activist citizens, such as those in the FICPM, are not defined juridically but by their creative engagement with developing the scene. The second principle in theorizing acts of citizenship is recognizing that the actors produced by the acts are oriented towards justice (ibid, p. 39). The third principle disrupts notions of legitimacy. As noted above, the acts performed by those involved in the FICPM are not necessarily founded in law and responsibility, but are still considered acts of citizenship. Isin argues that acts of citizenship often challenge commonly held beliefs about the law, therefore "acts of citizenship do not need to be founded in law or enacted in the name of the law" (ibid).

Although Peter Nyers' (2008) chapter "No One is Illegal Between City and Nation" centres non-status migrants and refugees as his objects of interrogation, I argue that FICP have been disappeared/shadowed in a similar way. Much like undocumented people's movements, FICP are leading the struggle surrounding issues of freedom and the range of social and civil rights currently denied to them. Nyers amplifies our understanding of agency and acts of citizenship by looking at how subjugated populations claim political subjectivity.

Similar to Isin (2008), Nyers (2008) disrupts common logic surrounding the question of who is eligible to make political claims and what constitutes a political act. The example he uses is people vocalizing their non-citizenship status. At the FICPM participants were asked to self-identify their status as FICP or as allies. A yellow wristband was given to allies and an orange band was given to FICP. One by one people stood up, declared their status and claimed their wristband. There are a few points that make this act significant.

First, this made people visible, which is not always safe and can be very intimidating in most settings. More pressing, however, is that by speaking one's status one asserts their agency and political subjectivity. Nyers (2008, p. 171) writes, "to self-identify as non-status [or in this case FICP] is to articulate a grievance to a community in which one has no legal or moral standing [...] the use of the term [FICP] can signal the emergence of a new political subjectivity". In other words, to demand rights such as voting, access to social welfare programs or education as a FICP and outsider to the body politic can be considered a political act that makes the actor (Isin, 2008).

FICP fall into an exceptional category of citizenship. Unlike undocumented people, many do have citizenship, but through FICP, we see that citizenship is not a guarantee of rights. FICP lack the full range of rights accorded to citizens. Additionally, they are denied the right to express themselves as political beings without fear of retribution and further marginalization.

Historically, racial difference in the United States has been managed violently. The measures of treating difference discussed in this paper were slavery, convict leasing, Jim Crow and mass incarceration. We see through these examples that a construct of citizenship that manages social difference only replicates and legitmates inequality. The FICPM is an example of an insurgent citizenship movement. The people involved in this movement are stepping out from the shadows with the express purpose of contesting their exclusions and challenging the current social order of rule and privilege. And on the theoretical terrain they are expanding current logics surrounding democratic citizenship.

In conclusion, zombiehood is a condition that no one is necessarily exempt from; it can, theoretically, happen to anyone exempted from the protection of the legal and political order. Once one inhabits this alternate form of death, it is difficult to attain reprieve – to be awakened from one's zombie condition. However, I contend that the aforementioned examples demonstrate that in the shadows, zombies have formulated an insurgent movement and are challenging, and sometimes destabilizing, long entrenched commonsense notions surrounding their nature and what they deserve. Their experience is the context and substance of a new urban citizenship. Despite the persistence of inequality, through their contestation, through their decision to engage the struggle, this mass population is writing themselves back into humanity.

ENDNOTES

[1] Two acronyms are used throughout this paper: FICP and FICPM. The former refers to formerly incarcerated and convicted people and FICPM refers to Formerly Incarcerated & Convicted People's Movement. I define convicted people as those populations who have been convicted of charges that place them under the supervision of the corrections system. This includes probation, parole, or any other court ordered system such as counseling or rehabilitation.

[2] I am invoking Ruth Wilson Gilmore's definition of racism in this paper. In *Golden Gulag* Gilmore defines racism as the state initiated technologies that differentially impact one population over another and consign them to early death. In reading about the evolution of the United States prison system it is apparent that people of colour have been disproportionately impacted by the PIC from the onset.

[3] According to the United States Sentencing Commission released 30 June 2011 Latinos have become the majority population in federal prisons. This is largely the result of prosecution of immigration offenses. To view the entire report consult: http://www.ussc.gov/Data_and_Statistics/Federal_Sentencing_Statistics/Quarterly_ Sentencing_Updates/USSC_2011_3rd_Quarter_Report.pdf

[4] For further information read Chapter 10 "Characteristics and Financial Circumstances of TANF Recipients" available at: http://www.acf.hhs.gov/programs/ofa/resource/ character/fy2010/fy2010-chap10-ys-final

[5] Critics of rights-based politics argue that this platform does little to challenge power structures. However, critical race theorists and feminist legal theorists such as Kimberle Crenshaw (1988) have posited that rights based claims though flawed can be reconceived to address the historical implications of denying rights to people of colour and women for instance. This argument acknowledges the shortcomings of legal rights in terms of eliminating oppressive structures and reinforcing individualism, but also recognizes the impact rights-based discourse can have on mobilizing marginalized populations to name what is killing them and begin to take active steps towards effecting change. Despite the limitations of rights-based claims I argue that dispossessed populations that articulate rights are demanding to be made legible and that these demands give them the possibility to rewrite themselves and perhaps even reimagine rights and/or the law.

[6] Orlando Patterson (1982) discusses social death extensively in *Slavery and Social Death.*

[7] Names of people in attendance at the conference such as the man in this example have been changed to protect their anonymity. Names of organizers and activists who are the public faces of this movement were not changed because their public stance and efforts have made them visible and searchable by name.

REFERENCES

Agamben, Giorgio (2000) *Means without End: Notes on Politics*, Minneapolis (MN): University of Minnesota Press.

Agamben, Giorgio (1998) *Homo Sacer: Sovereign Power and Bare Life*, Stanford (CA): Stanford University Press.

Alexander, Michelle (2010) *The New Jim Crow: Mass Incarceration in the Age of Colorblindness*, New York (NY): The New Press.

Arendt, Hannah (1968) *Imperialism*, in Engin Isin and Greg Neilson (eds.), *Acts of Citizenship,* London: Zed Books, p. 27.

Cacho, Lisa Marie (2012) *Social Death: Racialized Rightlessness and the Criminalization of the Unprotected*, New York (NY): New York University Press.

Camp, Jordan T. (2013) "Blues Geographies and the Security Turn: Interpreting the Housing Crisis in Los Angeles", *American Quarterly*, 64(3): 543 – 570.

Camp, Jordan T. (2009) "We Know This Place: Neoliberal Racial Regimes and the Katrina Circumstance", *American Quarterly*, 61(3): 693 – 717.

Crenshaw, Kimberle (1988) "Race, Reform, and Retrenchmen: Transformation and Legitimation in Antidiscrimination Law", *Harvard Law Review*, 101: 1331-1387.

Curtin, Mary Ellen (2000) *Black Prisoners and their World, Alabama 1865-1900*, Virginia: The University Press of Virginia.

Davis, Angela Y. (2005) *Abolition Democracy: Beyond Empire, Prisons, and Torture*, New York: Seven Stories Press.

Davis, Angela Y. (2003) *Are Prisons Obsolete?*, New York: Seven Stories Press.

Dayan, Colin (2011) *The Law is a White Dog: How Legal Rituals Make and Unmake Persons*, New Jersey: Princeton University Press.

Downey, Anthony (2009) "Zones of Indistinction: Giorgio Agabem's Bare Life and the Politics of Aesthetics", *Third Text,* 223(2): 109-125.

DuBois, William E.B. (1962[1935]) *Black Reconstruction in America 1860-1880*, New York (NY): The Free Press.

Escobar, Martha (2010) "Understanding the roots of Latina migrants' captivity", *Social Justice*, 36(2): 7–20.

Escobar, Martha (2008) "No One is Criminal", in *Abolition Now! Then Years of Strategy and Struggle Against the Prison Industrial Complex*, The CR10 Publications Collective (eds.), Oakland (CA): AK Press.

Feldman, Glenn (2004) *The Disfranchisement Myth: Poor Whites and Suffrage Restriction in Alabama*, Athens (GA): University of Georgia Press.

Formerly Incarcerated Peoples Movement (2011) Personal Audio Recording — November 2.

Garland, David (2001) *The Culture of Control: Crime and Social Order in Contemporary Society*, Chicago (IL): The University of Chicago Press.

Genty, Philip M. (2003) "Damage to Family Relationships as a Collateral Consequence of Parental Incarceration", *Fordham Law Journal*, 30(5): 1671.

Gilmore, Ruth W. (2007) *Golden Gulag: Prisons, Surplus, Crisis, and Opposition in Globalizing California*, Berkeley, CA: University of California Press.

Gilmore, Ruth W. (2002) "Fatal Couplings of Power and Difference: Notes on Racism and Geography", *The Professional Geographer*, 54(1): 15–24.

Gilmore, Ruth W. (1999) "Globalisation and U.S. Prison Growth: From Military Keynesianism to Post-Keynesian Militarism", *Race & Class*, 40(2/3): 171–188.

Glaze, Lauren (2009) "Correctional Populations in the United States, 2009", *Bureau of Justice Statistics, Bulletin.*

Gordon, Avery (2008) *Ghostly Matters*, Minneapolis (MN): University of Minnesota Press.

Greenfeld, Lawrence A. and Tracy L. Snell (1999) *Women Offenders*, Available at: http://www.ojp.usdoj.gov/bjs/abstract/wo.htm.

Harv. L. Rev., 101, 1331-1387.

Hill, Patricia (1990) *Black Feminist Thought: Knowledge, Consciousness, and the Politics of Empowerment*, New York (NY): Harper Collins.

Hooks, Bell (1984) *Feminist Theory: From Margin to Center*, Cambridge,(MA): Southend Press.

Isin, Engin and Greg Neilson G. (2008) "Theorizing Acts of Citizenship", in Engin Isin and Greg Neilson (eds.), *Acts of Citizenship*, London: Zed Books.

James, Joy (ed.), (2007) *Warfare in the American Homeland: Policing and Prison in a Penal Democracy*, Durham (NC): Duke University Press.

Kelley, Robin D. G. (2002) *Freedom Dreams: The Black Radical Imagination*, Boston (MA): Beacon Press.

Kousser, J. Morgan (1974) *The Shaping of Southern Politics: Suffrage Restriction and the Establishment of the One-Party South,* New Haven: Yale University Press.

Lacan, Jacques (1991) *The Seminar of Jacques Lacan, Book 1: Freud's Papers on Technique 1953-1954*, New York (NY): WW Norton & Company.

Laclau, Ernesto, and Chantal Mouffe (1985) *Hegemony & Socialist Strategy: Towards a Radical Democratic Politics*, Verso.

Law, Victoria (2011) "Reflections on the FICPM", *Tenacious: Art and Writings by Women in Prison*, Issue 24, Fall/Winter.

Law, Victoria (2009) *Resistance Behind Bars: The Struggles of Incarcerated Women*, Oakland (CA): PM Press.

Mancini, Matthew J. (1996) *One Dies Get Another: Convict Leasing in the American South 1866-1928*, Columbia (SC): University of South Carolina Press.

Mancini, Matthew J. (1978) "Race, Economics, and the Abandonment of Convict Leasing", *The Journal of Negro History*, 63(4): 339-352.

Marchevsky, Alejandra and Jeanne Theoharis (2000) "Welfare Reform, Globalization, and the Racialization of Entitlement", *American Studies,* 41(2/3): 235-265.

Meiners, Erica R. (2011) "Ending the School-to-Pipeline: Building Abolitionist Futures", *Urban Review*, 43: 547-565.

Neubeck, Kenneth J. and Noel A. Cazenave (2001) *Welfare Racism: Playing the Race Card against America's Poor*, New York: Routledge.

Nyers, Peter (2008) "No One is Illegal Between City and Nation", in Engin Isin and Greg Neilson (eds.), *Acts of Citizenship*, London: Zed Books.

Patterson, Orlando (1985) *Slavery and Social Death*: Harvard University Press.

Peck, Jamie and Nik Theodore (2008) "Carceral Chicago: Making the Ex-offender Employability Crisis", *International Journal of Urban and Regional Research,* 32(2): 251-81.

Peck, Jamie and Nik Theodore (2001) "Contingent Chicago: Restructuring the Spaces of Temporary Labor", *International Journal of Urban and Regional Research*, 25(3): 471-96.

Peck, Jamie and Nik Theodore (2000) "Work First: Workfare and the regulation of contingent labor markets", *Cambridge Journal of Economics*, 24(1): 119-38.

Perman, Michael (2001) *Struggle for Mastery: Disfranchisement in the South, 1888-1908*, Chapel Hill (NC): University of North Carolina Press.

Piven, Francis and Richard Cloward (1993), *Regulating the Poor: The Functions of Public Welfare*, New York (NY): Vintage Books.

Polakow, Valerie (1997) "Family Policy, Welfare, and Single Motherhood in the United States and Denmark: A Cross-National Analysis of Discourse and Practice", *Early Education & Development,* 8(3): 245-264.

Polakow, Valerie (1993) *Lives on the Edge: Single Mothers and their Children*, Chicago: The University of Chicago Press.

Prashad, Vijriv (2005) "Second-hand Dreams", *Social Analysis*, 49(2): 191-198.

Prison Activist Resource Center: Fact Sheets. African Americans and the Criminal Injustice System. http://www.prisonpolicy.org/scans/racism.pdf.

Rasmussen, Claire and Michael Brown (2002) "Radical Democratic Citizenship: Amidst Political Theory and Geography", in Engin F. Isin and Bryan S. Turner (eds.), *Handbook of Citizenship Studies*, Thousand Oaks (CA): SAGE, pp. 175-188.

Reilly, Bruce (2011) "Unprison. The Formerly Incarcerated & Convicted People's Movement Arises!" – March 21. Retrieved from http://unprison.com/2011/03/21/formerly-incarcerated-convicted-peoples- movement-arises/.

Rodrìguez, Dylan (2006) *Forced Passages: Imprisoned Radical Intellectuals and the U.S. Prison Regime*, Minneapolis (MN): University of Minnesota Press.

Said, Edward (1978) *Orientalism*, New York (NY): Pantheon.

Sandoval-Strausz, Andrew K. (2005) "Travelers, Strangers and Jim Crow: Law Public Accommodations and Civil Rights in America", *Law & History Review*, 23: 53-94.

Schram, Sanford F., Joe Soss, and Richard C. Fording (eds.). (2006) *Race and the Politics of Welfare Reform*, Ann Arbor (MI): University of Michigan.

Sexton, Jon (2010) "People-of-color-blindness: Notes on the Afterlife of Slavery", *Social Text*, 28 (2): 31-56.

Somers, Margaret (2008) *Genealogies of Citizenship: Markets, Statelessness and the Right to have Rights*, Cambridge (UK): Cambridge University Press.

Stratton, Jon (2011) "Zombie Trouble: Zombie Texts, Bare Life and Displaced People", *European Journal of Cultural Studies*, 14(3): 265-281.

Tenny, Elizabeth (2008) "Under Jim Crow's Thumb", *Cobblestone*, 29(4): 3-5.

Wacquant, Loic (2009) *Punishing the Poor: The Neoliberal Government of Social Insecurity*, Durham (NC): Duke University Press.

Wacquant, Loic (2005) "Race as Civic Felony", *UNESCO*, ISSJ 183.

Wacquant, Loic (2001) "Deadly Symbiosis: When Ghetto and Prison Meet and Mesh", *Punishment & Society*, 3(1): 95-134.

Walters, William (2008) "Acts of Demonstration: Mapping the Territory of (Non)-Citizenship", in Engin Isin and Greg Neilson (eds.), *Acts of Citizenship,* London: Zed Books.

Weisenburger, Steven (2005) "Bloody Sunday", *Southwest Review*, 90(2): 167-189.

Zucchino, David (1997) *Myth of the Welfare Queen*, New York (NY): Scribner.

ABOUT THE AUTHOR

Grace Gámez is a mother, activist and scholar. She is currently a doctoral student in Justice Studies at Arizona State University and expects to graduate in May 2015. Her research considers how formerly incarcerated and convicted mothers of colour, who are automatically written outside of the script of good mothers, navigate and negotiate their roles as parents with a focus on the afterlife of incarceration, probation and parole.

The Inside's Influence on the Outside
Grant Tietjen

To regret one's own experiences is to arrest one's own development. To deny one's own experiences is to put a lie into the lips of one's own life. It is no less than a denial of the soul.

– Oscar Wilde

INTRODUCTION

A professor whom I interviewed for a research project, having previously served many decades in prison, made a statement that I have internalized: "I am a criminologist who happens to be an ex-convict, not an ex-convict (ex-con) who happens to be a criminologist". The wisdom he imparted to me was the process of moving beyond the stigma of the ex-convict status and defining yourself by your subsequent accomplishments within academia, which in this individual's case was extensive. Yet, an issue that many ex-prisoners in the United States who have overcome nearly insurmountable obstacles to arrive at respected academic and professional positions must face is the enduring and nearly permanent social stigma placed upon those individuals with a felony conviction (Ross and Richards, 2003). Thus, the question I seek to ask is: how is my journey through the federal prison system and subsequent return to society defined for a formerly incarcerated academic, convicted of meth distribution during the height of the United States meth epidemic?

During the "meth (methamphetamines) epidemic", the already heavily burdened United States prison system swelled to epic proportions as correctional facilities filled with small-scale methamphetamine distributors and new prisons were constructed to contain the sudden influx of prisoners. Being convicted of meth distribution, I joined the incarcerated masses and then returned to society with a two-fold, educationally focused mission. First, how could I as an ex-prisoner gain a useful education, and second (this developed over the next five years after my release), subsequently use my education and life experiences to attempt to improve the life chances of other prisoners. Thus, through the use of auto-ethnographic methodology[1] (Ellis, 2009), I discuss how I define the journey from the street, to prison, back to the street, through graduate school, and to academia as a middle-class, white male convicted of a meth-related drug crime during the zenith of the United States meth epidemic (Reding, 2010; Semple *et al.*, 2008).

I examine how to apply my accrued experience to educational and pro-social endeavours and contrast my prison-to-academy journey with that of others in the Convict Criminology group. It is the responsibility of those who survived the prison system, and subsequently experienced a successful return to society, to educate and help others trapped in the de-habilitating confines of the criminal justice system find their way out.

Leaving "Out There"

As an ex-prisoner, I understand the scenario described above, yet before I learned about these experiences I had to undergo the transformation from a "citizen" to a "convict".[2] While incarcerated within several holding facilities and finally a federal prison camp on a journey that took me through four states (Nebraska, Kansas, Oklahoma, and South Dakota), I quickly learned to leave my old "citizen" self, or what I will refer to as the "out there" identity, behind, as it was replaced with my "inside" prison self. The process of the forced construction of a new identity is not easy and was certainly not undertaken without powerful internal and external consequences to me as an individual (Winnick and Bodkin, 2008; 2009). This experience redefined my life; I entered prison as an ignorant kid, yet would soon receive a crash course in the realities of social inequality and injustice that define the American criminal justice system. This is an experience common to many prisoners in the late modern system of mass incarceration (Ross and Richards, 2003), even across the ocean in a European country also experiencing record rates of incarceration. Crewe (2009, p. 35), when discussing the attitudes of modern prisoners in overcrowded British prisons, explains: "Among prisoners, perceptions of fairness and justice fell".

My experience as a former drug dealer, substance abuser, and subsequent drug offender, like many other ex-prisoners, happened in the midst of the War on Drugs (Jones *et al.,* 2009; Richards *et al.,* 2008; Tregea and Larmour, 2009) and the Meth Epidemic (Rasmussen, 2008; Reding, 2010; Semple *et al.,* 2008). Through my interaction with the correctional system, I quickly learned that the meth trade was largely a "white" phenomenon. Meth street and prison sub-culture incorporated many elements of rural/Midwestern/working-class American ideology, cultures that I was quite knowledgeable about, having grown up in a small Midwestern town and having worked on the family farm as a youth and in a welding shop in a small Midwestern city as an adult.

As a first-time prisoner who had never spent a previous day in a correctional facility, I quickly had to learn jail and prison cultural norms; then upon return to the street, I discarded my prison values/behaviours and re-conformed to life outside of the total institution (Goffman, 1961). Yet, prison had a powerful effect on me as an individual. Prisoners are different people when released from prison (Ross and Richards, 2003). The way I perceive reality has been negatively skewed, yet not without positive developments. The journey through a prison sentence taught me many lessons as a formerly incarcerated citizen, such as how to function under the complete control of others, the realization that social inequality is not just an abstract concept, and a firm belief that justice is not blind.

Suddenly, and without warning, I was extracted from society and placed in an environment that was completely foreign to me, an environment in which I would stay confined for the next two years as a federal prisoner. Thus, the immediate transition phase was a difficult process of adaptation. I divide this adaptation process up into two phases: the physical and the psychosocial adaptation phases.

Physical Adaptation Phase

Directly after arrest, I was placed in a local jail that also served as a federal holding facility. My initial reaction immediately after my arrest, when being booked into the county jail (which served as my holding facility while awaiting arraignment) was fear. I had never been in a correctional facility before. The clinically bright lights that reflect off of the concrete floors and blandly coloured walls found in any correctional facility, coupled with the loud noises of heavy steel doors slamming and echoes of prisoners yelling and bantering, came as quite a shock to me. I immediately began an intensive process of introspection, which lasted for months, searching out the inner depths of mind and consciousness for clues as to how I had arrived in this predicament. I was engaged in a process of soul searching.

As a prisoner, I had to learn to adapt to the strange and intimidating new conditions that jail presented to me. Because I was incarcerated as a first-time offender, I suddenly became aware of the loss of freedom that incarceration entails and went into an initial shock. I became numb to my environment in a sense, which retrospectively served as a temporary buffer/coping mechanism against the harsh realities of my environment. All of my movements were controlled by correctional officers and the institutional administration where

I was placed. As a prisoner, I was classified according to my offense type and previous criminal record. I had to ask to use the telephone, ask to move from one section of your facility to another, and ask for more personal items, such as toilet paper, shaving supplies and toothpaste.

Another startling realization was the loss of the amenities of home, such as comfortable furniture, hot showers and baths, limitless possessions, the ability to arrange your home the way you want, an automobile, choice of the food and clothing, privacy, and Internet access. Sykes (1958) presents these experiences as the "pains of imprisonment", outlining such phenomena as deprivation of liberty, loss of goods and services, deprivation of conventional sexual relationships[3], and loss of privacy and autonomy. I discuss these examples not as a subtle means of filing a complaint against the system, but to demonstrate the actual conditions within a federal holding facility. For any recently incarcerated prisoner, the physical surroundings shift drastically, and the process of adapting must be carried out quickly, as there is generally no way to avoid interacting with the physical environment when suddenly placed in a correctional facility outside of extreme measures (Clemmer, 1940; Irwin, 1970; Jones and Schmid, 2000).

PSYCHOSOCIAL ADAPTATION PHASE

This section will discuss the social and psychological components of adapting to prison life. Although this is a sociological paper, it is important to include the psychological experiences in the explanation of what incarcerated individuals' experience. The effect on self is a vital component when attempting to capture the prison experience. The social dynamic within prison often moves quite slowly and tends to be quiet and almost monastic in its monotony and routines. An issue that Hollywood simulations and sensationalized media reality shows fail to present when depicting prisons is the experience of boredom.

The vast majority of prison life is quite tedious and boring. Many prison facilities fail to provide adequate activities or employment to keep prisoners occupied (Elrod and Brooks, 2000). Prisoners are left to figure out how to fill up long hours of dead time without the resources to do so. Within prison, a strict daily routine must be adhered to, and deviation results in both formal sanctions from prison administration and often informal sanctions from other prisoners. Prisons bring large groups of people together in permanent close proximity who might not normally congregate together outside of a correctional facility, which eliminates the option of distancing oneself from stressful situations and threats of personal violence. Consequently, the potential for chaos and extreme social disorder is constant. Daily routines and schedules work to balance this equation out, creating some semblance of social order, but the grinding reality in regards to serving time in correctional facilities that commonly lack programs and activities for prisoners is to figure out what to do with *all* of that time.

As a prisoner, I quickly learned to show much more respect for personal space, always using proper manners and saying, "Excuse me" if I accidentally bumped into someone in a hallway, as not doing so could be interpreted as a personal insult or threat of violence. My ability to use diplomacy to talk my way out of potentially violent or dangerous situations without having to resort to physical or extreme measures became all the more important. I also quickly learned from other prisoners, that following the rules (outwardly) makes your stay in jail and prison much more bearable. As Crewe (2007, p. 272) explains when quoting a prisoner, "There's ways and means you can do everything you've got to do and not get into a confrontation. If you get into a confrontation you're an idiot in this day and age [...] There's ways of being passive but still assertive". Appearing to walk the line was the best method of staying off the guards' radar and avoiding disciplinary actions that would make my life quite miserable.

If conceptualized in abstract terms, the prison environment can be thought of as a waltz, with many moves and countermoves, somewhat similar to the outside world, yet perhaps with the addition of several more nuanced moves and countermoves. Each additional nuanced dance move within the correctional environment must be learned through the process of acclimation to this environment, while removing some "outside" dance moves from the process. When re-entering society, I had to determine which values (prison moves versus street moves) to keep and which values to discard (Irwin, 1970; Ross and Richards, 2003).

When released, the "street" (outside world) soon brusquely reminded me that the heightened state of manners, defensive behaviours, and cautious social interactions of the correctional sphere were not the normal state of informal everyday interaction. "Street" people will bump into you without a second glance, and proper manners, while practiced by some (and within formal situations), are not required, and one should not act surprised if they are not offered or practiced at all. Examples of this would be someone opening a door right in front of you and letting it shut in your face, not thanking you when you pick up something you saw them drop, and blatantly stepping in line ahead of you.

On the street, in most common social settings (barring some subcultures or countercultures), when a person does not follow through on a promise he has made to you, those actions do not result in threats or acts of violence. In prison, not following through on one's word is far more serious and has greater potential for severe repercussions, even violence. Within the correctional environment, owning property and large amounts of material possessions are not allowed. The total institutional environment acts as a levelling agent, taking away much of the value of pre-prison social status, thus "outside" traits that prisoners value must be redefined. As Goffman (1961, p. 16) explains when explaining the social and civil effects that prison wreaks upon the individual, "The inmate, then, finds certain roles are lost to him by virtue of the barrier that separates him from the outside world".

To be trusted, and considered an honest "stand-up guy" within the prison walls becomes a valuable asset, and to blatantly deviate from or not respect this behaviour places the individual prisoner in a very unstable position in relation to other prisoners (Irwin, 1970). This locates the dishonoured prisoner in a marginalized status in relation to the dominant prisoner population. Yet, it must be noted, that to conceptualize a prisoner population within a particular prison as a single body would be an oversimplification. Prisoner populations in modern prisons are comprised of multiple groups, affiliated by race, gang affiliation, religious groups, place of residence, and prisoners who choose not to be part of any groups (Irwin, 1987). The group demographics of individual prisons vary by several factors such as security level, location, state or federal facility, and type of administration that oversees the prison (Hunt *et al.*, 1993).

As discussed previously, the social dynamic within prison often moves quite slowly, tends to be quiet and almost monastic in its monotony and routines, and occurs within the majority of prison groups and across the boundaries of different groups. Most prison life is not as one-dimensional or violent as presented in mass media (Ross and Richards, 2003). Prison is actually a complex network of groups and intersecting social interactions. Most prisoners behave civilly most of the time. What must be expressed is that the total institutional setting itself, not the prisoners' intrinsic personalities, sets the stage for potential violent and extreme acts. Most prisoners, such as I was, are nonviolent men and women who simply want to serve their prison sentence and go home.

THE INSIDE

After sitting in federal holding facilities for ten months while traveling back and forth to court appointments, I finally received a sentence of two years in prison, three months in a federal halfway house, four years of supervised release, and three hundred hours of community service for a first-time nonviolent offence. During the ten-month court process, I was transferred to thirteen different federal holding facilities, moving from facility to facility for reasons unknown. Some of these lockups were county jails and smaller state facilities that the federal government contracted in order to hold the massive overflow of federal prisoners, and other facilities were private, for-profit prisons. The massive overflow of prisoners is due to the United States' war on drugs (Alexander, 2010; Austin *et al.,* 2001; Grey, 2001), which has played an integral role in generating the largest prison population in the world (Rose *et al.,* 2010).

It would be helpful to reference the previous ten months before I arrived in prison, when I was housed in county jails, private prisons, and federal holding facilities. Having been housed in five separate county jails for approximately ten months during the course of my federal sentence (some of these facilities multiple times), I can attest that serving jail time is a type of prisoner life that is far worse than prison time. Most people are surprised when I make this statement, yet the jail environment is far more stressful, less secure and more physically threatening than prison confinement (Irwin, 1985).

Within the county jail setting, federal prisoners and local prisoners are often housed together. Jails are often very dirty and quite crowded in comparison to most federal correctional facilities. As prisoners, we were held in very close quarters, with few amenities and even fewer diversions from boredom than within actual prisons. Many federal prisoners are housed in jails while awaiting court dates (as I was), such as sentencing hearings or the addition of new charges to their case. As such, the environment is often stressful. It is quite common for prisoners to receive news of new federal sentences, ranging from four or five years to a life sentence, or calls from wives wanting a divorce. Other stressors include losing their homes, property and children or being charged with additional crimes because witnesses from outside of jail are testifying against them in additional court cases.

Within this setting, emotions, depression and anger become intensified, as people must often deal with the worst news of their lives while confined in small spaces with individuals whom they often do not like or would never associate with outside of the correctional environment. This atmosphere culminates in a pressure cooker effect. I watched many prisoners reach their limits of patience with other prisoners or have nervous breakdowns as we were often powerless to handle the situations that were being presented to us. I wanted to cry on many occasions, thinking about spending the next several years of my life in prison, yet would only do so hidden away in a bathroom stall because I feared that others would take this as a sign of weakness.

FROM JAIL TO THE FEDS

Once the courts handed me my sentence, I was transferred by the Federal Bureau of Prison's (FBOP) very own airline (old, full-size passenger jets) staffed by air marshals to the Federal Transfer Center (FTC) in Oklahoma City, Oklahoma. The FTC facility holds several thousand prisoners and is unique in that the prisoners walk directly off the jet and into the prison via a skywalk. You are housed in "administrative population", which means that prisoners from all security classifications, from minimum to maximum, are housed together.

FTC was an environment of contradictions, full of stress and uncertainties. Many of us were awaiting sentencing verdicts or on our way to trial dates that could re-determine the entire course of our lives. Yet, within this environment I came into contact with many interesting people from all over the United States who had many stories to tell, and once you befriended them, they were surprisingly often happy to talk just to pass the time. Some encounters were often quite sobering, as I recall a hopeless looking younger prisoner sitting on a stairwell. As I walked laps around the second tier of the pod (housing unit) I was housed in, he randomly asked me where I was from. I responded that I was from Nebraska and asked him where he was from, and he despondently replied, "Nowhere".

Within the FTC, prisoners are often under a great deal of stress and deal with much uncertainty about their futures. Whereas, I had been in jails and federal holding for the ten months previous to arriving at FTC, many prisoners enter this facility as new recruits to the criminal justice system. Consequently, the facility's rules and guidelines are unknown to new prisoners. The FTC does not come with an instruction manual for prisoners, and many guards and prison staff are not willing to take the time to explain how the prison routine works. In this predicament, new prisoners are often disoriented and confused, and must attempt to rely on the advice of other prisoners (many of whom do not trust recently arrived prisoners), trial and error, and observing the routines of others.

Even with ten months of county jail experience as a prisoner, when I arrived at FTC, I was unable to immediately understand all of the rules of conduct and prison protocol within that facility. During "count", a specific time during the day when all prisoners are counted throughout the United States federal prison system, I was sitting on my bunk in my cell reading a book. A guard came to the window of my cell and suddenly became quite angry. He sternly barked that my bunkmate and I (a white-collar prisoner who had also just arrived at the facility) were to be standing up by our bunks. He quickly left and returned with his supervisor, the original guard wearing a sardonic smirk on his face. The supervisor, being a little less irate, sternly asked us if we had been here before, and both of us replied that we had not. We politely stated that we did not know we were supposed to stand, and the lieutenant, wanting to quickly be on his way, replied that, "Now we did". To elaborate, when counted, prisoners must stand and state their name and then their Federal Bureau of Prisons number, a number that once assigned, the prisoner generally never forgets.

While confined in this facility, my case was evaluated, and because I was a first time nonviolent prisoner, I was assigned a minimum-security (low security risk) status. Then, I was sent to a minimum-security prison in Yankton, South Dakota. Yankton Federal Prison Camp (FPC) is an all-male facility designed to hold around four hundred prisoners. Yet, at the time I arrived at FPC Yankton, the prison housed over six hundred prisoners due to prison overcrowding issues generated from the war on drugs. Rooms designed for four men were often crammed with six to eight men. As Yankton FPC was formerly a college in the early 1980s, the facility actually resembled a college campus, with many of the old stone and brick buildings registered with the South Dakota state historical society. The prison was located in the centre of town and encompassed several city blocks. Prisoners walked across town streets to access the cafeteria, drug treatment center and the gym facilities.

As a new prisoner, I was *processed* into the facility. To be processed as a human being is uniquely degrading process. As Garfinkle (1956, p. 421) states when describing successful degradation ceremonies, "I call upon all men to bear witness that he is not as he appears but is otherwise and in essence of a lower species". Many of the guards looked at me and the other prisoners with disdain, barking orders at us and acting as if talking to us somehow disgusted them.

My picture was taken, and I was issued an ID badge and a card that served as a debit card, allowing me access to any money I had in my commissary (prison store) account. I was informed of general prison rules and guidelines through mandatory introductory courses. Using my ID card, I could buy food, clothing and personal items, use vending machines, and purchase various random items such as notebooks and art supplies. I was given several pairs of khaki pants, shirts, belts, white undershirts, boxers, a pair of boots and socks. Running or walking shoes and workout clothes could be purchased at the prison store. In the winter, I was issued a coat, stocking cap and gloves.

Next, I was assigned housing, placed in a temporary dorm room before the prison staff could decide where to place me on a more permanent basis. After two weeks, I was assigned a room in a large dormitory style-housing unit (an old college administration building). Throughout this process, I was learning how to think and behave like an actual prisoner. Jail can only partially prepare someone for the prison experience, bringing the prisoner's reality into alignment with how to understand and exist within a confined space with limited resources and controlled physical movements (Irwin, 1985). The prisoner, when suddenly transported into the prison facility, comes into contact with many new experiences, rules and people, all of which are quite overwhelming to a first- time prisoner.

THE DORM

The dorm was located on the second floor of a large, rectangular, brick building. The centre of the dorm contained the restroom and shower facilities, laundry rooms, microwaves for people to cook their own prison store food, and a couple of reading rooms for prisoners to study and read in. At one end of the hall were two large TV rooms, and at the other end of the hall was a game room with pool tables and vending machines. The dorm held approximately one-hundred-and-sixty prisoners. We slept in bunk beds, with older, disabled and long-term prisoners often occupying the lower bunks, while the younger, more physically able and "short-timers" (prisoners with shorter sentences) occupied the top bunks.

TO FIND A JOB

Once housed, it was up to me to seek out a prison job. There were several options, such as the maintenance shop, the grounds-keeping shop, baking and cooking training programs within the kitchen, and the electrical shop. Prisoners could apply for apprenticeship programs within these shops. Generally, only prisoners with longer sentences were accepted to such apprentice programs because the programs required several thousand hours of work on the job to complete the apprenticeship process successfully. Jobs could be found in many places, such as working as a custodian (orderly) in one of the prison dorms or shops. Short-term prisoners such as I were more likely to find work in more monotonous jobs, like dishwashers, custodians or clerks.

After a few inquiries, I found a job as a custodian for the maintenance shop. While the pay was meagre – eleven cents per hour – I was fortunate to have a supervisor who was a fair and decent man. The daily eight-hour workload consisted of one to two hours of sweeping, mopping, buffing and polishing per day, and then the rest of the day was spent attempting to look busy and staying under the guards' radar. I often spent time reading or doing homework when I had enrolled in college correspondence courses towards the end of my prison sentence.

INTERACTION WITH THE HELP

As a new prisoner, I quickly learned that keeping contact with guards to a minimum was necessary if I was to have a semi-pleasant stay in prison. Some mandatory contact was unavoidable, such as at count times, at the workplace and during counselling sessions. Each prisoner is assigned a caseworker/counsellor who reviews your case files, determines your progress while incarcerated and implements any changes that will be made to your status as a prisoner. Changes to prisoner status potentially included an increase in security status due to violent behaviour, a decrease in security status due to good behaviour or determining which required correctional programs you were to enrol in. Yet, outside of these limited required interactions with staff, prisoners who followed the rules were respectful and avoided conflict with other prisoners generally reduced their contact with guards.

Within a minimum-security facility, incidents of violence are quite infrequent in comparison to that of higher security prisons, as violent prisoners are not allowed to serve time in minimum-security facilities. Prisoners with a history of violence are generally housed in higher security facilities, such as maximum-security United States penitentiaries (Maghan, 1999), and prisoners whom the federal courts designate as ultra-violent or dangerous are housed in super-maximum security facilities, such as the

ADX in Florence, Colorado (Briggs *et al.*, 2003). The average minimum-security prisoner is intelligent enough to realize that the conditions in camps are far less severe and far more desirable than in higher security prisons such as medium lows, medium highs, and maximum securities (federal penitentiaries), where violence, fighting, gang conflict and poor housing conditions are far more common.

THE PEOPLE ON THE INSIDE

Within prison, compared to jails, there is a shift in the average type of prisoner. Men in prison have often been convicted of more serious offenses, due to the felony charge that is necessary to end up in this environment. Yet, most prisoners are convicted of nonviolent offenses (e.g. persons convicted in relation to prohibited drugs). Many of the men in prison have very colourful personalities and are intelligent individuals with incredibly diverse life histories, ranging from dark and depressing stories of abuse and violence to gallant stories of traveling the world and wild adventures. My intention is not to project that prison is always a positive and exciting environment but to relay that the prison environment, and prisoner culture is far more complex and full of nuance than is often portrayed in the sensationalized versions of prison presented in mass media.

It must be stated that there are differences in prisoners between different prisons. The prison I was housed in was a minimum-security facility with only a decorative fence to separate us prisoners from the rest of the world. Of course, the first question I receive when telling others this fact is, "Couldn't prisoners just walk off?" In a word, yes. If a prisoner wanted to escape, he would need only walk out of the prison yard and into the surrounding town and attempt to disappear. To do so added five to seven extra years to his sentence and resulted in a transfer to a far higher security, harsher prison with no chance of return to the lower security camp. In the fourteen months I was housed at Yankton no one attempted to escape and I heard of only one attempted escape that occurred several years before I arrived, in which a middle-aged, white-collar prisoner attempted to walk away from Yankton with only two years left on his sentence after he found out that his wife was having an affair with his attorney. The man was spotted walking through a neighbouring town by a prison guard who happened to reside there. He was promptly re-captured, returned to a higher security prison and assigned an additional five years onto his remaining sentence.

THE FEDERAL PRISON

Within federal prisons, average prison sentence lengths vary by race, with African Americans serving an average of 105 months and whites serving an average of 62 months, a 41 per cent difference in length (BJS, 2002). Minimum-security federal prisons receive many white-collar prisoners and prisoners who are nonviolent, first-time criminalized persons, many who come from slightly higher socio-economic backgrounds than other prisoners and have somewhat higher mean levels of education (Braithwaite, 1985). It is generally accepted among prisoners that a federal prison is a better facility to be confined in when compared to state facilities, which are often dirtier, have less educational and work programs (Crayton and Reusteter, 2008), often have fewer amenities, are poorly funded, and are generally of lesser quality (being older and/or cheaper in construction). The scales, however, tip in favour of state institutions when discussing the issue of sentence length. Federal prisoners often serve longer average sentences than state prisoners, with the average federal felony sentence being 61 months (BJS, 2003) and the average state felony sentence being 27 months (Wright, 2006) due to mandatory-minimum sentencing guidelines (Hofer and Semisch, 1999) and truth-in-sentencing legislation (Shepherd, 2002).[4]

Within the average minimum-security FPC, there are greater concentrations of white-collar prisoners, with many of them coming from wealth and privilege previous to incarceration. When housed in my permanent dorm in Yankton, my first bunkmate was formerly a lawyer from a large metropolitan area, raised in a wealthy political family, a graduate of a prestigious law school and a published author all before he arrived in prison. Several of my fellow dorm mates were formerly medical doctors, lawyers, and accountants, had PhDs or were successful businessmen. One was even a former Chicago police officer. The prisoners housed at Yankton FPC came from all over the United States, with an additional sprinkling of prisoners hailing from foreign countries.

There was some visible resentment generated by prison staff, focused on the wealthier and more highly educated prisoners, many of whom would enter and leave prison millionaires and who already possessed more experiences than most people would gather in multiple lifetimes. Many of my evenings and afternoons in the prison's central yard were spent chatting with such prisoners about those experiences. Hanging out and engaging in such conversations lent many new perspectives to my own previously limited worldview.

Within Yankton FPC, the prison allowed a well-known outside public speaking group, Toastmasters International, to form a prison-based chapter, "The Gavel Club". This speaking group was run by prisoners and only attended by prisoners, the staff generally leaving us to do as we saw fit. I served as the group's secretary and prisoners took turns speaking each week. Occasionally, we were allowed to bring in outside speakers, such as local historians or local people of interest. This venue allowed for interesting discussion and opportunities for prisoners to hear the stories of people whom they might never come into contact with outside of this setting.

One of the prisoners, an accountant and wealthy businessman serving time for a white-collar offense, having previously served on a presidential accounting committee, spoke about the large, hotel real estate trade. Another prisoner, a former medical doctor, spoke about his medical practice, while many other prisoners spoke about their life histories and gained valuable experience in public speaking. From this venue, the often negative backdrop of prison life was transformed into a positive one, allowing prisoners to gain life skills such as public speaking, while concurrently learning about alternative worldviews, different cultures, and the personal backgrounds of their fellow prisoners. It provided a much needed refuge from the often chaotic and boring nature of prison life.

RECONNECTING WITH EDUCATION

After many long months of sitting in county jails with little or no access to formal educational opportunities, the prison allowed me to participate in correspondence courses. Such courses had to be paid for at my own expense, as no educational funding or grants are now available to prisoners due to the elimination of Pell Grants to state and federal prisoners after 1994 under the Omnibus Crime Control Act (Welsh, 2002). This legislation was enacted because of the misconception that huge sums of money in the form of Pell Grants were being handed to prisoners, when in actuality, the savings gained by eliminating the grant were virtually negligible (ibid).

I settled on two sociology courses (my discontinued college major from many years before prison) offered by a large, Southern university. I used funds from a small savings account to pay tuition costs and soon received my textbooks and course materials in the mail. The prison provided study rooms, access to typewriters for homework and essay assignments (no computer access at this time), and proctors who would preside over my exams when needed.

Yankton FPC was considered a showcase prison within the federal prison system because of its relatively nice facilities and grounds, and unique educational department that offered the prisoners the opportunity to attain associate's degrees in business, science or horticulture through a local college. The local college, a Catholic institution, was instrumental in operating the college programs and keeping the educational department at Yankton, having advocated on behalf of the prisoners many times when the prison administration had threatened to eliminate the educational program. While this program was technically available to me, I did not participate in it because my stay at Yankton would not have been long enough to finish all of the required courses and I had already completed enough college credits to be ranked as a junior in college (at a western Nebraska community college and at the University of Nebraska) previous to incarceration.

THE TRANSITION

Often the former prisoner experiences an amalgamation of both pre-prison and prison identities, as s/he picks up many mannerisms and behaviours within prison, such as survival skills, how to navigate and talk one's way through difficult or dangerous situations, and how to interact with diverse groups of people. When the prisoner is released, some of these traits are transported to the outside world. Depending on the specific type of behaviours, traits and mannerisms the former prisoner learned, how these skills and behaviours are applied to everyday interactions in the outside world will determine whether such skills will be a benefit or a detriment to the newly released ex-prisoner (Jones and Schmid, 2000).

When re-entering society, the prisoner must attempt to "un-prisonize" himself, following what some scholars refer to as a U-shaped pattern of prison socialization (Wheeler, 1961; Garabedian, 1963; Jones, 2003). Within this pattern, I attempted to internalize prison culture upon entry into the prison and then divorced myself from prison culture when I returned to the streets, an incredibly difficult task that I initially struggled with. De

La Cruz (2012, p. 143), an ex-prisoner scholar speaks very eloquently to this issue: "As much as I hated to admit it, all those street freedoms had meant very little to me. After all, if staying out had been so important why did I always manage to return to the penitentiary? I clearly had become institutionalized". Having journeyed through the criminal justice system several times before beginning his educational journey, De La Cruz sums up a common experience that many ex-prisoners experience: having difficulty transitioning to the chaotic streets from the very predictable routines of the correctional institution.

While I only served one prison sentence before beginning the journey to higher education, many of the courageous men and women I have met through the Convict Criminology (CC) group have had similar journeys, having served multiple prison sentences before finding the pathway to scholarship and academia, thus overcoming incredible odds.[5]

In addition, my journey from the prison to the streets differed from other CC members from the perspective of my middle class background's providing more resources and support than that of many other ex-prisoners upon my release. Newly released from prison, Richard Hendricksen similarly speaks of being fortunate in comparison to many of his fellow prisoners when describing the initial months on the street: "I often felt a mixture of unearned security and guilt for simply having a room, a roof over my head, food in the kitchen, or that my mother could lend me ten or twenty dollars when I needed it from her tips she brought home from work until I found a job" (Hendricksen and Mobley, 2012, p. 115).

Many of my fellow ex-prisoner scholars and acquaintances have overcome not only prison, but also poverty, substance abuse, racism, and physical and psychological abusive family backgrounds. Thus, their journeys are nothing short of incredible demonstrations of courage, steady ambition and strength of human spirit. This emphasizes that the difficulties of the shift from the mind numbing prison to the realities of society are experiences that society and family members of prisoners should be sensitive to.

THE "REAL WORLD"

Walking out of the confines of the minimum-security prison and back into the hectic pace of society was a shock to my prison-dulled "outside world" senses. As a prisoner, I forgot the nuances of everyday life, such as the smell of cologne or perfume or the ability to go somewhere anytime without asking permission or filling out the proper paperwork. The bright lights and fast pace of everyday society is, at first, quite overwhelming.

With a felony conviction, ex-prisoners must often "out" themselves to employers, even though a large percentage of crimes harm no one but the individual doing it (Ross and Richards, 2003; West and Sabol, 2010). For example, 22 per cent of prisoners in state and federal prisons are convicted of nonviolent drug-related offenses (UCR, 2000). Additionally, ex-prisoner academics and ex-prisoners in general are forced into a position in which they must defend actions that took place in the distant past, even in the face of mounting evidence that after several years (six or seven) have passed without subsequent criminal convictions, the potential that an ex-prisoner will re-offend is reduced to the same level as those without criminal convictions (Kurlychek and Bushway, 2006).

I quickly learned that most job applications contain "the box" that asks for prior criminal convictions, which must be checked if any chance of employment is to be gained. If I checked the box, then I was often asked to explain myself once again, as if I were in a recurrent cycle of being re-convicted for an offense that I had committed many years ago. Yet, I had already repaid my societal debt through the process of incarceration, community service and probation (supervised release in the federal prison system).

In addition to the initial sensory overload and stressors that everyday society imposes on the ex-prisoner, comes the permanent changes that prison life has imprinted onto your general worldview, social mind and psyche. This phenomenon is often overlooked, as society expects us as ex-prisoners to immediately re-acclimate to the outside world as if nothing life-altering has happened. However, for me as a newly released ex-prisoner, I perceived the world differently. I now know what it is like not to exist in the eyes of my own culture, to be treated as a societal non-entity, to truly be nothing more than just a number in a long sequence of numbers, and to have your humanity taken away from you.

THE SHIFT TO SCHOLARSHIP

By December 2005, I had navigated through two years of coursework, finishing my bachelor's degree. I caught the attention of some of the professors in the sociology department who strongly recommended that I apply for graduate school. I took their advice and was accepted into the University of Nebraska's sociology graduate program a year later. Also, towards the end of my bachelor's degree studies, I began to develop a strong interest in crime and deviance research, and in early 2005, I presented at a large, regional, sociology conference in Minneapolis, where I fortunately made contact with the CC Group which would alter the course of my life.

To explain further, Convict Criminology is group of criminologists who share the common bond of past incarceration, and/or a strong interest in critical, progressive, reform based criminological research and criminal justice policy. The CC group strongly believes in the power of mentorship and provided me with guidance and advice throughout the course of my graduate career. The CC group also places a heavy emphasis on research collaboration among members. The focus is the production of viable, relevant scholarship and publications, which is vital to the furthering of CC's mission of creating an academic space for formerly incarcerated academics' voices to be heard, critically examining the massive social inequalities present in the current American criminal justice system, and formulating progressive/rehabilitative correctional policy (see Jones *et. al.*, 2009; Richards and Lenza, 2012).

The coursework for my master's degree began in the fall semester of 2007. When I had been in graduate school for a couple of years and more fully understood how the academic world operated, I began to mentor the newer members of the CC group, providing advice and encouragement in regards to navigating graduate school applications, how to properly approach the academy in regards to securing future employment, and increasing marketability as formerly incarcerated academics.

I received my PhD in sociology in May 2013. My dissertation examined the educational pathways of formerly incarcerated academics/professionals from prison to academia. During the course of my graduate career, I have had the opportunity to travel extensively to conferences, study abroad, and conduct research in both in the United States and in Europe. In June 2010, the CC Group, in collaboration with KRIS of Finland and Tampere University, organized the International Scientific Conference on Global Perspectives on Re-entry at Tampere, Finland (see Ekunwe and Jones, 2011).

In the summers of 2009 and 2011 and in the winter of 2012-2013, I traveled to Scandinavia, spending time in Sweden and Denmark, and was

allowed to visit a Swedish halfway house and criminal/drug rehabilitation
clinics and make contact with KRIS, a Swedish advocacy group for formerly
incarcerated people that now has many international locations. Through my
travels, I was able to make contact with formerly incarcerated people who
would lend their expertise to my dissertation research and gain a valuable
cross-national perspective on other more progressive, non-punitive, and
rehabilitative forms of criminal justice policy and corrections.

DISCUSSION

Within this auto-ethnographic study, I re-examine and attempt to understand
life experiences I have accumulated during the journey into incarceration,
through incarceration, and my subsequent release and educational journey
to academia. Auto-ethnography allows me to focus on the correctional and
educational systems through my own cultural lens. My journey was not
an easy path. While I must recognize the many socio-cultural advantages
that I possessed (i.e. supportive family, as well as economic and social
resources), the journey from no prior criminal record to the federal prison
system within a matter of days was a brutal experience. Undergoing a
complete loss of my former identity and subsequently being processed
through the doorway of "out there" into the crushing pervasiveness of the
total institution brought me to my knees (see Garfinkle, 1956; Goffman,
1961). I was confused and lived in despair, oscillating between feeling as
if the world had somehow forgotten me and that a great mistake had been
made. I kept repeating to myself, "How did I get here?" The impact of
this experience has had far-reaching positive and negative effects on the
rest of my life, even twelve years from my initial arrest date and ten years
since my release from prison.

From a positive perspective, through a process of soul searching, I
determined that the purpose of the remainder of my life was to return to and
work within education in some capacity. My ideas and plans began to take
further shape as the months and years passed by in prison, and I was able to
bring these ideas to fruition as explained in "The Real World" section above.
I became motivated to help others find their way from prison to education
as a means of improving their general quality of life and decreasing their
chances of return to prison. Overall, this journey has exceeded my wildest
expectations, as I have not only had the opportunity to meet some of the

most inspirational people and engage in fascinating research, but actually watch as research and educational groups I am participating in are making real pro-social changes in the lives of the formerly incarcerated, many of whom are now my good friends, even if it is often the slow process of reaching one person at a time.

Future research could examine the educational experiences that women prisoners incarcerated during the meth epidemic encountered in the federal prison system and upon their release. A further qualitative examination of how social class and race affect the process of higher education within prison and post-release could provide much needed insight into how the forces of social inequality interact with prisoners seeking out education. Such qualitative research could provide the much needed and often overlooked human component to influence progressive, educationally-based, criminal justice policy, especially in light of strong evidence that education reduces recidivism (Berman, 2008, Pettit and Western, 2004).

Additional policy implications include providing increased educational resources, such as funding for currently incarcerated and recently released prisoners, and encouraging more prisoners and ex-prisoners to focus on higher education. Subsequently, employers should be encouraged to offer realistic opportunities for viable employment to ex-prisoners upon attainment of higher educational credentials, based on the positive outcomes that many experience when provided realistic opportunities to do so (Richards and Ross, 2001; Schmidt, 2002; Terry, 2003).

CONCLUSION

The process of imprisonment has left its scars upon my life, as I struggle with issues of anxiety, self-doubt and depression. As mentioned at the beginning of the paper, I entered the prison system as a hard drug abuser (methamphetamines and cocaine), but I am now in recovery. Yet, this is a life-long issue that is part of me and my journey to prison, through prison, and through my educational experiences. Hard drug abuse led me to endure some of the darkest points in my life, yet my subsequent recovery has allowed me to experience the best parts of my life. In addition, prison permanently restructured the way I view the world. I must contend with the permanent stigma of a felony record that follows me for the rest of my life, existing at times as a dark shadow from my past, waiting to wreak potential havoc upon my life, to snatch away what few precious accomplishments I have had the opportunity to attain through the advocacy, generosity, and mentorship of many great people whom I will never be able to fully thank for their help.

While some people may brand this fear as irrational, to me, it is a persistent dread that I must struggle with one day at a time. Yet, it is my duty to inform all of the newly released formerly incarcerated people that I become acquainted with about my experiences and provide mentorship to them. I explain to these individuals the message that over time and with a commitment to higher education, life can improve – that there is a way out. If I do not help my fellow formerly incarcerated peers, my education and unique experiences serve no purpose, and that would be an injustice in and of itself.

ENDNOTES

[1]   I chose the auto-ethnographic method due to my experience as a formerly incarcerated individual (a.k.a. ex-con), I needed a research methodology that would allow me to examine my experiences and construct meaning out of my observations. Auto-ethnography provided this venue. As Ellis (2009) states: "…reexamining the events we have lived through and the stories we have told about them previously allows us to expand and deepen our understandings of the life we have led, the culture which we have lived, and the work we have done".

[2]   I must note that I do not currently define myself as a convict (or other labels such as prisoner or felon), because of the negative social stigma that society attaches to words such as convict, prisoner and felon. When referring to others who have been confined in prison, I personally refer to them and myself as formerly incarcerated individuals.

[3]   Sykes refers to loss of heterosexual relationships. Yet, I refer to deprivation of conventional relationships of both hetero- and homosexual nature, because even through homosexual relations can and do take place within the correctional setting, these relationships take on a different form, distorted by the uniquely closed/desperate environment presented in the prison total institution (Goffman, 1961).

[4]   Although the *average* federal sentence is greater, the actual time spent for specific crimes can be much longer at the state level. Homicide, rape, and armed robbery, which usually fall under state jurisdictions, generally carry the possibility of a sentence of life without parole, and many states, not only the federal government, also have mandatory minimum sentences for specific crimes.

[5]   A group of formerly incarcerated criminologists/criminal justice scholars, sociologists, and non-convict scholars who collaborate with us.

REFERENCES

Alexander, Michelle (2010) *The New Jim Crow,* New York (NY): The New Press.

Austin, James, Marino A. Bruce, Leo Carroll, Patricia L. McCall, and Stephen C. Richards (2001) "The Use of Incarceration in the United States: ASC National Policy Committee White Paper (Executive Summary)", American Society of Criminology National Policy Committee, *The Criminologist,* 26(3): 14-16.

Berman, Douglas A. (2008) "Reorienting Progressive Perspectives for Twenty-First Century Punishment Realities", *Harvard Law and Policy Review Online,* 3: 1-20.

Braithwaite, John (1985) "White Collar Crime", *Annual Review of Sociology,* 11: 1-25.

Briggs, Chad S., Jody L. Sundt and Thomas C. Castellano (2003) "The Effect of Supermaximum Security Prisons on Aggregate Levels of Institutional Violence", *Criminology,* 41: 1341-1376.

Chambliss, Bill (1972) *A Professional Thief's Journey: As Told and Edited by Bill Chambliss,* New York (NY): Harper & Row Publishers.

Clemmer, Donald (1940) *The Prison Community,* New York (NY): Holt, Rinehart and Winston.

Crayton, Anna and Suzanne Rebecca Neusteter (2008) "The Current State of Correctional Education Paper to be presented at the Reentry Roundtable on Education", *Prisoner Reentry Institute,* John Jay College of Criminal Justice.

Crewe, Ben (2009) *The Prisoner Society: Power, Adaptation, and Social Life in an English Prison,* New York (NY): Oxford University Press.

Crewe, Ben (2007) "Power, Adaptation and Resistance in a Late Modern Men's Prison", *British Journal of Criminology,* 47: 256-275.

De La Cruz, Jesse (2012) "Detoured: My Journey from Darkness to Light", *Journal of Prisoners on Prisons,* 21 (1&2): 139-145.

DeRosia, Victoria R. (1998) *Living Inside Prison Walls: Adjustment Behavior.* Westport (CT): Praeger Publishers.

Ellis, Carolyn (2009) *Revision: Autoethnographic Reflections on Life and Work,* Walnut Creek (CA): Left Coast Press.

Elrod, Preston and Michael T. Brooks (2003) "Kids in Jail", in Jeffrey Ian Ross and Stephen C. Richards *(eds.), Convict Criminology,* Belmont,(CA): Thomson Wadsworth, pp. 325-346.

Ekunwe, Ikponwosa O. and Richard S. Jones (eds). (2011) *Global Perspectives on Re-Entry.* Tampere (Finland): University of Tampere Press.

Garfinkle, Harold (1956) "Conditions of Successful Degradation Ceremonies", *American Journal of Sociology,* 61: 420-424.

Goffman, Erving (1961) *Asylums: Essays on the Social Situation of Mental Patients and Other Inmates,* New York (NY): Doubleday.

Grey, James P. (2001) "Why Our Drug Laws Have Failed and What We Can Do about It", in *A Judicial Indictment of the War on Drugs,* Philadelphia (PA): Temple University Press.

Hendricksen, Richard and Alan Mobley (2012) "A Tale of Two Convicts: A Reentry Story About the Impacts of Ethnicity and Social Class", *Journal of Prisoners on Prisons,* 21(1&2): 105-118.

Hofer, Paul J. and Courtney Semisch (1999) "Examining Changes in Federal Sentence Severity: 1980-1998", *Federal Sentencing Reporter,* 12(1): 12-19.

Hunt, Geoffrey, Stephanie Riegel, Tomas Morales, and Dan Waldorf (1993) *Changes in Prison Culture: Prison Gangs and the Case of the "Pepsi Generation",* Social Problems, 40(3): 398-409.

Irwin, John (1987) *The Felon,* Berkeley (CA): University of California Press.

Irwin, John (1985) *The Jail: Managing the Underclass in American Society,* Berkeley (CA): University of California Press.

Jones, Richard S. and Thomas J. Schmid (2000) *Doing Time: Prison Experience and Identity Among First-Time Inmates,* Stamford (CT): Jai Press Inc.

Jones, Richard S., Jeffrey Ian Ross, Stephen C. Richards, and Daniel S. Murphy (2009) "The First Dime: A Decade of Convict Criminology", *The Prison Journal,* 89(2): 151-171.

Kubrin, Chris E. and Eric A. Stewart (2006) "Predicting Who Reoffends: The Neglected Role of Neighborhood Context in Recidivism Studies", *Criminology,* 44(1): 165-197.

Kurlychek, Megan C. and Shawn D. Bushway (2006) "Scarlet letters and Recidivism: Does an Old Criminal Record Predict Future Offending?", *Criminology and Public Policy,* 5: 483-504.

Maghan, Jess (1999) "Dangerous Inmates: Maximum Security Incarceration in the State Prison Systems of the United States", *Aggression and Violent Behavior,* 4: 1–12.

Pettit, Becky and Bruce Western (2004) "Mass Imprisonment and the Life Course: Race and Class Inequality in U.S. Incarceration", *American Sociological Review,* 69: 151-169.

Rasmussen, Nicholas (2008) "America's First Amphetamine Epidemic 1929—1971", *American Journal of Public Health,* 98: 974-985.

Reding, Nick (2010) *Methland: The Death and Life of an American Small Town.* New York, USA: Bloomsbury.

Richards, Stephen C. and Michael Lenza (2012) "Editors' Introduction: The First Nickel and Dime of Convict Criminology", *The Journal of Prisoners on Prisons,* 21(1&2): 3-15.

Richards, Stephen C., Donald Faggiani, Jed Roffers, Richard Hendricksen, and Jerrick Krueger (2008) "Voices from Prison", *Race/Ethnicity: Multidisciplinary Global Contexts,* 2: 121-136.

Richards, Stephen C. and Jeffrey Ian Ross (2001) "Introducing the New School of Convict Criminology", *Social Justice,* 28(1): 177-190.

Rose, Chris D., Victoria Beck and Stephen C. Richards (2010) "The Mass Incarceration Movement in the USA" in Martine Herzog-Evans (ed.), *Transnational Criminology Manual, Vol. 2,* Nijmegen (The Netherlands): Wolf Legal Publishers, pp. 533-551.

Ross, Jeffrey Ian and Stephen C. Richards (eds.) (2003) *Convict Criminology,* Belmont (CA): Thompson Wadsworth.

Sampson, Robert J.and John H. Laub (2005) "A Life-Course View of the Development of Crime", *The ANNALS of the American Academy of Political and Social Science,* 602(1): 12-45.

Schmidt, Peter (2002) "College Programs for Prisoners, Long Neglected, Win New Support", *Chronicle of Higher Education* – February 8.

Semple, Shirley J., Jim Zians, Stephanie Strathdee and Thomas L. Patterson (2008) "Methamphetamine Using Felons: Psychosocial and Behavioral Characteristics", *The American Journal of Addiction*, 17: 28-35.

Shepherd, Joanna M. (2002) "Police, Prosecutors, Criminals, and Determinate Sentencing: The Truth about Truth in Sentencing Laws", *Journal of Law and Economics*, 45 (2): 509-533.

Sykes, Gresham, M. (1958) *The Society of Captives,* Princeton (NJ): Princeton University Press.

Terry, Charles M. (2003) "From C-Block to Academia: You Can't Get There from Here", in Jeffrey Ian Ross and Stephen C. Richards (eds.), *Convict Criminology*. Belmont (CA): Thompson Wadsworth, pp. 95-119.

The Sentencing Project (no date) "The Federal Prison Population: A Statistical Analysis". Retrieved from (http://www.sentencingproject.org/doc/publications/inc_federalprisonpop.pdf).

Tregea, William and Marjorie Larmour (2009) *The Prisoners' World: Portraits of Convicts Caught in the Incarceration Binge,* Lanham (MD): Lexington Books.

United States Crime Rates 1960-2009. FBI, Uniform Crime Reports.

Welsh, Michele F. (2002) "The Effects of the Elimination of Pell Grant Eligibility for State Prison Inmates", *Journal of Correctional Education,* 53: 154-158.

West, Heather and William Sabol (2010) "Prisoners in 2009" (PDF). Bureau of Justice Statistics.

Winnick, Terri A. and Mark Bodkin (2009) "Stigma, Secrecy and Race: An Empirical Examination of Black and White Incarcerated Men", *American Journal of Criminal Justice,* 34: 131-150.

Winnick, Terri A. and Mark Bodkin (2008) "Anticipated Stigma and Stigma Management Among Those to be Labeled 'Ex-con'", *Deviant Behavior.* 29: 295-333.

Wright, Ronald F. (2006) "Federal or State? Sorting as a Sentence Choice", *Criminal Justice,* Summer. Retrieved from http://sentencing.nj.gov/downloads/pdf/articles/2006/Sept2006/document05.pdf.

Zamble, Edward and Frank J. Porporino (1988) *Coping, Behavior, and Adaptation in Prison Inmates,* New York (NY): Springer-Verlag.

ABOUT THE AUTHOR

Grant Tietjen is an Assistant Professor in the Department of Sociology and Criminal Justice, with a concentration in Criminal Justice studies, at St. Ambrose University in Davenport, Iowa. He completed his Ph.D. and undergraduate studies at the University of Nebraska – Lincoln in 2013. His general research interests include criminology with a focus on penology, criminological theory, class inequality, and education. More specifically, his recent work examines education in correctional and post-incarceration settings. His pedagogical interests include criminological theory, deviance, cross-national justice studies, and drug usage and society.

Actually Innocent Prisoners: Will the State Get it Right?
Mwandishi Mitchell

In September of 2011 a Report of the Advisory Committee on Wrongful Convictions came down through the General Assembly of the Commonwealth of Pennsylvania. The Advisory Committee, made up of a who's who of political big shots, with names like Edward Marsico Jr., the District Attorney of Dauphin County, Seth Williams, the District Attorney of Philadelphia, and David Rudovsky, a prominent civil rights attorney proposed legislation that would curb the travesty of wrongful convictions. The forty-eight team panel, with John T. Rago, Esq. sitting as its chair, put together a three-hundred-one page dossier on wrongful convictions in Pennsylvania and other states. The dossier focuses on the main causes for wrongful convictions such as eyewitness identification, electronic recording of custodial interrogations, post-conviction relief, legal representation, science, and for those who prove their innocence, redress.

Pennsylvania Senator Stewart J. Greenleaf spearheaded this movement years before with the introduction of Senate Bill No. 381 in 2006. At that time eight individuals were exonerated in Pennsylvania through post-conviction DNA testing, three of which were incarcerated for murder and one of whom was on death row (Garis, 2003). The Advisory Committee also cites this important fact:

> Since 1989, 34 states and District of Columbia have been witness to 273 post-conviction DNA exonerations. These exonerations represent cases in which the conviction has been indisputably determined to be wrong by continuing advances in the use of DNA science and evidence. They represent tragedy not only for the person whose life is irreparably damaged by incarceration for a crime he did not commit, but also for the victim since each wrongful conviction also represents the failure to convict the true perpetrator (p. 1).

Reading that had me feeling that at least some in the Pennsylvania Legislature felt my pain. I have spent ten years in a Department of Corrections prison cell for a wrongful conviction. You would think this news brightens my spirits, but it does not. I know all too well the politics involved in some cases of wrongful convictions. The *quid pro quo* factor will leave many of us here languishing in agony.

As it stands in Pennsylvania, DNA testing is not a right pertaining to wrongfully convicted prisoners. My own petition for DNA testing has been denied by the trial court. The Advisory Committee seeks to make DNA testing a right by amending the current statute to clarify: 1) the right to petition for DNA testing post-conviction and 2) that DNA test results be compared to profiles in the state DNA database pre- and post-conviction.

To put it bluntly, an innocent defendant convicted of a crime becomes an innocent victim himself. They will sit for years on end in some prison cell with all hope of being exonerated lost. When you are in a prison environment, anything can happen to you. Imagine stepping out of your cell on your way to chow and someone slamming a homemade "shank" into your gut over a petty argument from two nights prior or, even worse, being beaten down to the ground by institutional staff for any reason they are able to come up with to justify their actions. These are the things that could happen to an innocent inmate on "Any Given Sunday".

Wrongful convictions are not some new phenomenon in Pennsylvania, or any other state, but the point is it happens, and when it does, states should be responsible and compensate the wrongfully convicted with redress. Under the current existing law, most of the individuals who are freed after being found innocent of the crimes for which they were convicted are unable to obtain any compensation from government or other sources for the losses they sustained. The Advisory Committee settled on three main areas for consideration: 1) financially compensating the wrongly convicted; 2) providing transitional services for those released; and 3) establishing a commission to review cases of those found to be innocently convicted, so that the Commonwealth can learn from its errors and prevent them from happening again.

The Advisory Committee recommends that the Commonwealth statutorily compensate any person who is released from imprisonment due to a wrongful conviction. Under the current proposal, the Committee agrees on a payment of $50,000 a year for each year the wrongfully convicted had to spend in jail. But honestly, can anyone put a price on you being deprived of your liberty? Of course not. In Pennsylvania, only four of the eleven individuals exonerated by way of post-conviction DNA testing received compensation. There is something wrong with that picture.

For wrongfully convicted prisoners, there is a tough, rough road ahead. Even after being exonerated, the mental stress and pain takes a toll. You have to adapt to civilization after decades of being locked away. Things as simple as operating a cell phone will require extreme thought and patience.

Personally, I am tired of waiting for Pennsylvania to catch up with the rest of the country. Just across the Delaware River in New Jersey, the attorney general has sole authority over all law enforcement personnel in that state. He has mandated new procedures to crack down on witness identification procedures (nearly 75 percent of wrongful convictions are due to eyewitness misidentification) by using National Institute of Justice guidelines (Innocence Project, 2013). To the West in Ohio, the legislature has adopted statutes that require administrators who oversee perspective witnesses in line-ups and photo arrays remain ignorant of whether or not a particular defendant is present (LAWriter, 2010). Each witness views each folder individually. For each folder, the witness must state whether or not the picture is of the perpetrator and his or her confidence in that identification.

Also, we need the help of the public as well. They vote for the politicians who make the laws of this nation. Many have stereotypical views of prisoners in general, like if the justice system has problems, the pros will fix them; everyone in prison claims to be innocent; an eyewitness is the best evidence; our system almost never convicts an innocent person; it dishonours the victim to question a conviction; only guilty people confess; conviction errors get corrected on appeal; and, the worst, wrongful convictions result from innocent human error.

To the thirteen Pennsylvania exonerees, I salute you. Matthew Connor, Bruce Nelson, Jerry Pacek, Jay C. Smith, Dale Brison, Vincent Moto, Willie Nesmith, William Nieves, Edward Baker, Steven Crawford, Bruce Godschalk, Thomas Kimbell, Jr., and Nicholas Yarris.

The rest of us are still waiting for the Pennsylvania legislature to pass the recommended Advisory Committee legislation.

REFERENCES

Innocence Project (2013) "Eyewitness Misidentification". Retrieved from http://www. innocenceproject.org/understand/Eyewitness- Misidentification.php?gclid=CKr0op nTjLoCFc6e4AodNlQAmg.

Garis, Jeff (2003) "Exoneration of Pennsylvania death row prisoner anticipated Tuesday; Death penalty moratorium supporters to hold vigil at courthouse", *Death Penalty Information Center* – December 8. Retrieved from http://www.deathpenaltyinfo.org/ node/136.

LA Writer (2010) *Administration of Photo or Live Lineups, Section 2933.83*, Ohio Revised Code. Retrieved from http://codes.ohio.gov/orc/2933.83.

Joint State Government Commission (2011) "Report of the Advisory on Wrongful Convictions", Harrisburg (PA): General Assembly of the Commonweatlth of Pennsylvania, September. Retrieved from http://jsg.legis.state.pa.us/resources/documents/ftp/documents/9-15- 11%20rpt%20-%20Wrongful%20Convictions.pdf.

ABOUT THE AUTHOR

Mwandishi Mitchell continues to fight in court in pursuit of overturning his wrongful conviction. He is also a contributing writer for *Minutes Before Six*, a blog for death row writers and those serving life without parole. He can be contacted at:

Mwandishi Mitchell #GB6474,
P.O. Box 244,
SCI Graterford,
Graterford, PA 19426,
USA

How, Why, and About What Do Federal Prisoners Complain: And What We Can Do About It

Miguel Zaldivar *

INTRODUCTION

Federal prisoners[1] spend a large part of their day complaining about prison conditions. In fact, complaining about things such as meals, commissary and boredom is a major pastime for the bulk of the Federal Bureau of Prisons (BOP) population. However, what many of my fellow prisoners fail to grasp is that they sometimes contribute to the very prison conditions they complain about.

That current and former prisoners embellish their crimes and prison experiences is well documented. Not only is the average Joe behind bars inclined to telling colourful "war stories", but also convict authors such as Edward Bunker, Jack Abbot and Michael Santos have sensationalized their writings for what is known in the literary world as "effect". These raconteurs have done an exceptional job of selling the now infamous "convict bogeyman", and are in part responsible for the myths surrounding crime and corrections (Ross, 2008, p. 17).

Granted, other groups such as the mass media have also contributed to the unsavoury views society holds of crime and corrections (ibid). However, the majority of these groups are not immediately privy to what life behind bars is "really" like. These outlets often rely on the prisoners they report on and profit from their information. Unfortunately, the prison anecdotes passed on to these groups are often sensationalized for either a few dollars or minutes of fame. Thus, it seems ironic that those prisoners who have endured the sting of the correctional beast continue to promote images of crime and corrections that are not only deleterious to their own well-being, but also to the future survival of more than 2.3 million men and women behind bars (Fathi, 2011).

In this auto-ethnographic paper I first highlight three important and interrelated prison conditions prisoners complain about – crowding, staff members and other prisoners. These conditions not only negatively affect prisoners and staff members, but also threaten the security and orderly running of an institution. Second, I argue that prisoners are among the primary creators of this environment. By succumbing to the Convict Code's way of life, prisoners fetter their personal development and compound the odds of becoming recidivists. Their return trip to the penitentiary exacerbates the very conditions they complain about. Lastly, I provide what I believe to be the most efficacious solution available to my fellow prisoners. After twenty-four years of incarceration, I find that pointing to external circumstances for our troubles is a waste of time. Scholars and prisoner authors have long expounded on the injustices of the criminal justice system. Yet, as evident by the rising number of prisoners and the exorbitant rate of recidivism, the body of work of these well-intentioned individuals has accomplished little. Therefore, we must stop waiting on others to do for us what only we can do for ourselves. It is time we start taking responsibility for our past behaviour, as well as our present and future well-being.

OVERVIEW

In his benchmark study, *The Society of Captives: A Study of a Maximum Security Prison*, Gresham Sykes (1958) warns against discussing the prison experience from a collective prisoner perspective. With uncanny perspicacity, Sykes points out that each prisoner develops a unique interpretation of life behind bars. He suggests that, due to the individualized needs and backgrounds each prisoner brings to the institution, it can be "argued that in reality there are as many prisons as there are prisoners" (ibid, p. 63). Despite this caveat, however, Sykes exposes the existence of a "hard core of consensus expressed by the members of the captive population with regards to the nature of their confinement" (ibid). Bearing this understanding, I advance my observations of life within the walls and razor-wired fences of the Federal Bureau of Prisons.

The public may find it difficult to believe that a relatively small group of prisoners not only dictates, but also defines, "what is" and "what is not" acceptable prison behaviour. Nevertheless, the sad reality is that through peer pressure, the threat of or use of violence, and the corrupt tenets of the Convict Code,[2] a small, self-interested group of prisoners not only terrorizes the general prison population into submission, but also perpetuates a prison culture that devours the men who are ensnared in its web. Indeed, the tentacles of the Code are so overwhelming that even white-collar criminals begin walking, talking and acting like hardened convicts within a short period of entering a federal prison. Truly, the time frame in which the transformation from "fish" to "convict" takes place is frightening.

However, in most cases, the transmutation is nothing more than a convenient façade. The majority of prisoners succumb to the Convict

Code way of life not because they actually metamorphosed into hard-core prisoners, but rather because: 1) the Code allows prisoners to passively and safely express discontent over prison conditions; 2) it provides a historical (and some would say credible) podium from which to pass on embellished "war stories"; and 3) it offers a safe haven from the more predatory elements of the general prison population. The latter of these motivates most prisoners to adopt the Code's tenets as quickly as possible because they fear that failure to do so may result in them being ostracized, being labeled a "rat" and, in some extreme cases, being physically and/or sexually assaulted.

In sum, I have witnessed how through peer pressure, the use of violence, and the corrupt tenets of the Convict Code, a relatively small group of prisoners, consisting of less than ten percent of the prison's population and composed primarily of active gang members, coerces the general prison population into acting and behaving in ways that perpetuate the very prison conditions prisoners complain about. Ironically, what the vast majority of prisoners fail to grasp is that by succumbing to the Code's way of life, they are fueling the criminal incubator that not only breeds their present prison conditions, but also threatens their future freedom.

CORRECTIONAL JOURNEY

My correctional journey commenced outside of the United States. In 1988, I spent eight hellish months at Her Majesty's Prison (a.k.a. Fox Hill) in Nassau, Bahamas. Then shortly after being released from Fox Hill, I was held for five tormenting months at El Reclusorio de Hermosillo, Sonora, Mexico. These distinctly different experiences not only left lasting impressions, but also educated me on how debasing prison life can be and provided the correctional acumen to navigate the rough years that were soon to come.

My walk with the BOP began on May 9, 1990, and ever since then I have been a studious, but reluctant, guest of the federal prison system. I am a nonviolent, first-time offender serving thirty years for conspiracy to import, possess and distribute over ten tons of cocaine. And even though I forced the government into not one but two district court trials and appealed both my cases all the way to the United States Supreme Court, today, after many years of soul searching, I make no bones about admitting I am guilty of the charges brought against me.

While in the custody of the BOP I have been housed in four United States Penitentiaries (Leavenworth, Florence, Atlanta and Coleman 1), two

Federal Correctional Institutions (Edgefield and Coleman-Medium), three Federal Detention/Transfer Centers (Miami, Tallahassee and Oklahoma), one Medical Center for Federal Prisoners (Springfield), and numerous city and county jails from as far west as Salt Lake City, Utah, to the southeast shores of Broward County, Florida to the capital's sordid D.C. Jail.

Shortly after arriving at USP Leavenworth (October 1991), I realized life behind the wall is all about making choices; I could either "click up" and waste the next twenty-five years of my life, or I could invest in myself and pursue a college education – I chose the latter. During my incarceration, I have earned two baccalaureate degrees from regionally accredited universities.[3] I have completed over fifty cognitive/behavioural programs and educational courses. Since 2003, I have been a Suicide Companion, and from 2002 to 2006, I was a speaker for FCC Coleman USP1's Community Outreach Program. In addition, I spent seven years in the BOP's Skills Program working and living with "special needs inmates". During those years, I mentored and tutored emotionally and psychologically disturbed prisoners, mediated problems among participants, and facilitated courses such as Criminal Thinking Elimination, Breaking Barriers, Victim Impact and Stinky Thinking. Through these experiences, I learned a great deal about the BOP, my fellow prisoners and myself. However my trek with the BOP has also experienced hiccups along the way.

Throughout my incarceration, I have spent nearly five years in Special Housing Unit (SHU), more commonly known as "the hole". Some of those "time outs" I deserved, such as for my 1991 ill-advised and disastrous escape attempt from the Metropolitan Correctional Center in Miami, Florida, while others were thrown upon me due to no fault of my own. For example, while at USP Leavenworth, I was placed in SHU over a fictitious escape plot contrived by a disgruntled BOP captain. After a number of refusals to remove me from the High Accountability Security Program, I decided to go over the captain's head. The assistant warden of custody agreed with my request and instructed the captain to take me off the program. I quickly realized I had won the battle, but lost the war.

In retaliation, within six weeks I was thrown in SHU and transferred to another institution. In fact, the fallout from this incident led to my continuous detention in SHU for over two years while being transferred through three different institutions and eventually returned to where I started, at USP Leavenworth. But regardless of why I ended up in SHU, the experience and savvy-ness I gained from those excursions are priceless.

In short, throughout my correctional journey, I have been an avid student of my environment, as well as of the men and women I interact with daily. I am what some people call an "insider", well-versed as to what life behind bars is really like.

CROWDING

Over the last three decades, living conditions in the BOP have significantly deteriorated. Long gone are the days when federal prisoners lived in sparsely populated cellblocks, enjoyed palatable meals and bragged about well-stocked commissaries. Today, federal prisoners are fortunate if they are not tripled bunked, find a few vegetables in their meals, and are able to purchase seasonal fruits from commissary every now and then.

Several interrelated factors account for the overall difficulties consuming the BOP. For example, budgetary cuts, high employee turnover rate, and lower hiring standards. Yet, probably no single factor is more salient than the crowded conditions plaguing the federal prison system.

Crowding has various causes. For example, the Sentencing Reform Act of 1984 (SRA), which launched the Federal Sentencing Guidelines, introduced mandatory minimums, decreased good-time awarded, and eliminated parole for federal prisoners, is blamed for the overcrowded conditions ravaging the BOP (Fathi, 2011). In addition, stringent and punitive community supervision policies have also received much attention for their contributions to the crowding enigma (Richards and Jones, 2004). Therefore, to argue that these juridical and administrative determinants have not played significant roles would be puerile.

Be that as it may, these factors are beyond the immediate control of any single prisoner and to continue complaining about these factors does not appear to have ameliorated the crowding situation. On the contrary, blaming external circumstances not only frees prisoners from accepting responsibility for their contribution to the problem, but also hinders them from taking corrective action. Indeed, the blame game solidifies the "victimhood" mindset that compounds the likelihood of prisoners becoming recidivists, which in turn exacerbates the crowded conditions they complain about. However, there is one decisive factor prisoners do have control over that can alleviate, or at least contain, the crowding problem – the exorbitant rate of recidivism.[4]

Recidivism is an animal that has been studied and assailed from every angle imaginable. Yet, over the last four decades no meaningful reduction in the rate of this beast has been achieved. On the contrary, the rate of recidivism has steadily risen throughout the years.

There have been two major studies conducted on recidivism over the last forty years. The first looked at 108,580 men and women who were released from prison in 1983 (Beck and Shipley, 1989), and the second tracked 272,111 former prisoners released in 1994 (Lagan and Levin, 2002). Both studies used similar methodology and followed the participants for the same extended period after release – three years. That these studies reached analogous conclusions is startling. However, even more alarming is the fact that the rate of recidivism rose five percentage points over a mere eleven year period – from 62.5 percent in 1989 to 67.5 in 2002 (Langan and Levin, 2002). If we extrapolate this number over the last twenty years, we can easily say the rate of recidivism is fast approaching the eighty percent mark. Granted, this is an overly simplistic view of an extremely complicated phenomenon. Nevertheless, the point here is not to dwell on the mechanics of said conclusion, but rather to emphasize the fact that the deck is stacked against prisoners when it comes to making a successful re-entry.

That recidivism is a major contributor to prison crowding is a no-brainer. The fact that four out of ten prisoners are re-arrested within one year of being released and seven out of ten within three clearly underscores this point (Langan and Levine, 2002, p. 3). Yet, little is heard regarding this link. Why are people so reluctant to connect the dots? The BOP's prison population consists of a 35/65 split between first-timers and repeat criminalized persons (FPP: A Statistical Analysis), which means that out of the more than 220,000 federal prisoners at least 150,000 are recidivists. These facts should be enough to convince even the most ardent opponents of this reality. Still, few scholars are willing to examine this link. Convict authors conveniently overlook the issue and individuals who mean well, find it un-American to hold the recidivist accountable for his or her contribution to the crowding equation. In fact, some members of these groups go as far as to portray recidivists as mere victims of a callous and punitive judicial system, and argue that crowding is the product of "the structural realities of prison conditions and re-entry[...] and not the criminal or deviant behaviour of individuals" (Richards and Jones, 2004, p. 202). These scholars de-emphasize the fact that recidivists, like all members of free society, are legally responsible for their actions and have ultimate say-so over the decisions they make.

Are there exceptions to this socially accepted convention? Of course there are. The mentally incompetent, for instance, are held to a less rigorous legal standard (*Cooper v. Oklahoma*, 1996). This, in most cases, allows them to receive special treatment from the criminal justice system. A case in point is that of my older brother, Roly, who only served six months in a federal medical facility instead of the twenty years he would have done if he had not be declared mentally incompetent to stand trial. However, in my experience, I have found that the overwhelming majority of recidivists (and prisoners in total) are fully cognizant of the decisions they make. But regardless of one's position on this matter, the fact remains that to ignore the recidivist's role in the crowding riddle is not only irresponsible, but also foolishly dangerous.

Crowded prison conditions affect much more than the sleeping arrangements and meals of the prisoner population. Indeed, crowded conditions not only trigger most of the problems/issues staff must deal with on a daily basis, but also ignite the majority of the difficulties prisoners complain about (Ross, 2008).

The effects of crowding are felt long before the institution reaches its maximum rated capacity (Allen, 2004). In general, crowding leads to less educational, vocational, and recreational opportunities for the prison population. Also, crowding means there are less institutional jobs available, leaving a large number of prisoners with little to do. This idleness induces boredom and generates a great deal of frustration (Ross, 2008). And one thing is certain – bored and frustrated prisoners are dangerous prisoners. In fact, "the rate of death, suicide, homicide, inmate assault, and disturbances increase as prison population density increases" (Allen, 2006, p.169). Moreover, this finding holds regardless of whether prisoners are "confined in maximum, medium, or minimum security" institutions (ibid).

Crowded prison conditions also affect the little things prisoners must deal with daily. For example, crowding means prisoners have less access to things such as telephones, computers, televisions, showers and even visiting privileges. These little things may seem trivial, but a large number of prisoner/prisoner assaults arise over such petty things as the use of a telephone or the changing of a television channel. Furthermore, these incidents not only are happening more frequently, but also are evolving into more serious confrontations as "homeboys" and gang members get dragged into the mix.

Lastly, crowded prison conditions lead to greater health risks for both staff and prisoners. Diseases such as tuberculosis and hepatitis are easily transmitted. Crowding not only facilitates the spread of these diseases, but also makes them very difficult to treat since it is impossible to isolate infected prisoners when there is no place to put them (Ross, 2008).

In short, there is no doubt federal prisoners have a legitimate complaint when it comes to the crowded prison conditions pillaging the BOP. Crowding not only makes prison life more challenging, but also exposes both staff and prisoners to extremely dangerous situations. Unfortunately, this prisoner complaint garners little public or government sympathy because the complainers themselves are major contributors to the crowding situation. By choosing to re-offend and/or violate conditions of supervised release and returning to prison, whether in the face of structurally difficult life circumstances or not, recidivists encumber the crowded conditions they complain about. Granted, as highlighted above, other factors such as the Sentencing Reform Act of 1984, the Federal Sentencing Guidelines, and the stringent community supervision policies enforced by probation and parole agencies have also significantly contributed to the overcrowding conditions. Nevertheless, these juridical issues are beyond prisoners' control, and for us (prisoners) to keep blaming them for the crowded conditions we endure without accepting, or at least acknowledging, our contribution to the problem is problematic.

STAFF MEMBERS

Staff is a subject of much discord and entertainment among prisoners. Prisoners enjoy maligning staff and complaining about lazy case managers, antagonistic correctional officers (COs) and incompetent work supervisors. If you let prisoners tell it, you would think a bunch of cretins and simpletons run the BOP. Yet, in fairness to these prisoners, the BOP does employ its share of all of the above. Still, the negative perception prisoners have of staff cannot be adequately explained by the employment of a few bad apples – other factors are at work here.

Over the last fifteen to twenty years, staff's treatment of prisoners has lapsed considerably. There are several reasons for this. For example, the BOP has experienced an exodus of its most qualified and educated personnel. Too many top-tier employees have abandoned the BOP for more challenging, better paying and less stressful jobs. In addition, budgetary cuts have coerced the BOP into "pushing out" senior staffers who earn higher wages than incoming employees do in similar positions. These factors have the Feds scraping the bottom of the barrel for potential hires and have forced the BOP to operate its facilities with less qualified and experienced CO's.[5]

Other factors affecting prisoners' perception of staff are the result of the staff problems/issues mentioned earlier; specifically, less educated and experienced staff lack the skills to properly manage unruly prisoners. Furthermore, throughout the last decade I have witnessed how understaffing not only has exacerbated the problem, but also has become the Achilles' heel of the BOP.

To make up for staff shortage, the BOP is forcing officers to work longer hours and to man more than one post at a time. For example, at FCC Coleman – Medium COs are frequently pressed into working "doubles", that is, back-to-back shifts. In fact, understaffing is so prevalent at FCC Coleman that posts are not even manned unless they are considered "mission critical"[6]. Add to this the responsibility of supervising more than one housing unit at a time, and one begins to understand why COs are more irritable and less willing to deal with prisoner nuisances. This situation has created a great deal of stress, cynicism and even deviance as COs cut corners to get their jobs done, generating a host of complaints from the prisoner population. Thus, these factors not only compromise the safety and orderly running of the institution, but also affect prisoners' perceptions of staff.

With this said, are prisoners' complaints regarding lazy case managers, antagonistic COs, and incompetent work supervisors grounded in facts or are prisoners just maligning staff because it is the "convict" thing to do? Before answering this question, it is worth remembering that life in prison is all about perception. Unfortunately, the perception of most prisoners is skewed by the omnipresence of the Convict Code. To illustrate how the Convict Code warps prisoners' perception of staff members and other prison complaints, let us examine a common occurrence I have endured since May 2006.

FCC Coleman-Medium announces prisoner "work call" at 7:30 a.m. Over the public address system (PA), the entire prison population is treated to the sound of, "Work-call, Work-call. All inmates up the middle, shirt tails tucked in, I.D.'s out". To get to my work assignment, I, along with approximately 400 other prisoners, have to travel a distance that is twice as long as the return trip back to the housing units. This is because instead of turning right at the first available sidewalk leading to UNICOR, kitchen, facilities, education, and the like, we are made to walk "up the middle" (straight ahead) toward the compound shack where several officers watch us parade by, making sure our shirt tails are tucked in and that we display our prison identification cards. This exercise takes place every weekday morning (excluding holidays), rain or shine. Therefore, one would think that after several weeks of this, prisoners would deduce that this routine is not going to change regardless of the amount of complaining they do. Yet, the outcries invariably begin as soon as we approach that first available right.

As we near the first intersection, some prisoner will say something to the effect of, "This is fucking ridiculous. It makes no fucking sense to walk all the way around". Then someone else will add, "These assholes (staff) are on a power trip. Bet these bitch-ass motherfuckers pull rank here because they can't do it at home". Of course this badmouthing of staff generates some laughter and several "Ain't that the truth", along with other similar forms of agreement. This nonsense goes on for the eighty or ninety yards leading up to the compound shack; from there, these rants become more personal.

As we approach the compound shack, from somewhere along this moving queue we hear, "There is that punk Smith", referring to Officer Smith.[7] Then someone else will say something like, "You know he likes to feel you up when he shakes you down". And sure enough, as we walk past the staff members, Officer Smith singles out some prisoner who for whatever reason believes that the instructions announced over the PA system do not apply to him. At this point, with hundreds of prisoners watching, Officer Smith orders the transgressor to turn around and proceeds to pat him down. Consequently, this scene corroborates the views regarding Officer Smith that have been heard by a large number of prisoners. Thus, after several days of listening to this verbal garbage and witnessing similar scenes, it comes as no surprise that the vast majority of prisoners internalize vituperative views of Officer Smith. Before you know it, through rumours and innuendos, Officer Smith is perceived as an antagonistic CO who also harbours homosexual tendencies.

However, let us sprinkle a sense of reality to the above events by briefly addressing the following questions: 1) What purpose does complaining about and/or disparaging Officer Smith serve? 2) Who benefits the most from this prison ritual? 3) How does it affect the general prison population?

The most salient purpose behind the grousing and decrying of staff members is a prisoner's need to be accepted by his peers. While the human need for social acceptance is natural and instinctive, in prison this becomes a counterproductive and destructive force. Moreover, by voicing his discontent, a prisoner hopes to dispel any thought of him being weak and expatiates the belief that his show of solidarity against Officer Smith will keep the predators off his back.

The prisoners who benefit the most – at least from a prison culture perspective – are those who belittle staff on a regular basis. The majority of prisoners perceive these vocal individuals as the "bad asses" of the compound, the ones who do not give a damn about rules and regulations. In effect, by constantly speaking out and engaging in confrontations with staff, these prisoners climb up the distorted and, in my experience, quite delusionary hierarchical structure of the Convict Code.

Finally, the general prison population is affected in several ways. However, none is more pernicious than the cunning fashion in which it is coerced into acting and behaving in ways that support the views of the most stentorian complainers, who usually are self-proclaimed adherents of the Convict Code. This leads many prisoners to adopt attitudes, habits, beliefs, and expectations that are counterproductive to their present well-being and future freedom. For many prisoners, either out of peer pressure or the threat of and/or use of violence, succumbing to the Code's way of life is a means of surviving the prison experience and to be accepted by their peers. Unfortunately, what most prisoners fail to grasp is that said way of life not only fetters their personal growth while incarcerated, but also compounds the odds of them becoming recidivists. Simply put, the attitudes, habits, beliefs and expectations that function in a prison setting are not transferable to the free world. Moreover, these inimical prison attributes do not just magically transform and/or vanish as prisoners walk out the front door. In fact, I suspect that it is precisely the attitudes, habits, beliefs and expectations that prisoners nurture while incarcerated that land 7 out of 10 of us back in prison within three years of being released.

Therefore, after peppering a healthy dose of reality into the mix, it is easy to appreciate how the Convict Code skews prisoners' perception of staff members and other prison complaints. Most prisoners complain about lazy case managers, antagonistic correctional officers, and incompetent supervisors because they believe it is expected of them since it is perceived as the convict thing to do, and not because a bunch of cretins and simpletons run the BOP. Still, to deny that the BOP employs all of the above would miss the mark.

In summation, the Convict Code facilitates three important functions: 1) the Code allows prisoners to passively and safely express discontent over prison conditions; 2) it provides a historical podium from which to pass on embellished war stories; and 3) it offers a safe haven from the more predatory elements of the prison population. Accordingly, prisoners tend to complain about staff members simply because most believe it is expected of them. Complaining about lazy and incompetent staff not only provides a safe way of expressing frustration over prison conditions, but also allows prisoners to play up the "convict" role in the presence of their peers. Through their complaints, prisoners express solidarity and, more importantly, display their allegiance to the Code.

Prisoners complain about staff members for a number of reasons. However, probably no reason is more salient than a prisoner's desperate need to fit into a hostile environment that preys on weakness and individuality. The BOP does employ a number of lazy, difficult and incompetent staff members. And, unfortunately, the number of these shady employees will continue to rise as the BOP lowers its hiring standards. However, until this small minority becomes at least a majority of one, it behooves us not to mislead the public. Besides, exaggerating staff's shortcomings is not going to alleviate our present living conditions. On the contrary, it can only make matters worse.

OTHER PRISONERS

Complaining about other prisoners is natural in a prison setting. Think about it. Anytime thousands of men are thrown together in a confined space and forced to interact differences are going to arise. However, over the last ten to fifteen years, complaints regarding other prisoners have soared. Several factors account for the increased grumbling. Yet, the most conspicuous is the fact the BOP has been housing a more criminally diverse clientele.

Up until the mid 1990's, the BOP's prison population consisted of the "cream of the crop" of the underworld: international drug traffickers, upper echelon organized-crime members, professional thieves and white-collar criminals. During that time, the majority of prisoners were well-educated and many were multilingual with worldly experience (Richards, 2005, p. 189). The type of crimes these men typically engaged in were in line with what criminologists refer to as "rational" and "instrumental" (Brown, *et al.*, 2004, p. 29). In addition, prisoners of old not only tended to be conscientious in their dealings with others inside, but also were cognizant of the possible consequences their behaviour provoked from both staff and others who are incarcerated.

In contrast, many of today's BOP prison population is made up of uneducated, ill-mannered, and incorrigible petty criminals. This new generation of criminals tends to engage in "expressive" and *"mala in se"* type of crimes (ibid, p. 28). Not only do they lack the education and manners of their predecessors, but they also enjoy engaging in prison behaviour that is both irritating and dangerous to other prisoners. But, before addressing some of these behaviours, it is worth emphasizing three factors that account for the overall discrepancies between the prisoners of old and those of this new generation.

First, over the last twenty-five years a large number of crimes that once were under the bailiwick of local and state governments have been federalized (Ehrlich, 2000). During this period, I have noticed that an increasing number of men have entered the federal systems for crimes such as crack jacking, sexual offenses and small quantities of drugs. Historically, local and state governments have pursued these types of crimes. However, from the increased presence of these prisoners, it is obvious that the federal government has been vigorously prosecuting crimes it once regarded outside of its judicial purview. Second, the closure of the District of Columbia's correctional system pushed nearly 15,000 prisoners into the BOP (Washington Post, 2006).

The majority of these men are serving sentences for an assortment of crimes ranging from first-degree murder to petty theft. Moreover, the arrival of D.C. prisoners introduced into the BOP a variety of quirks unlike anything the feds had ever experienced. From my interaction with these men, I have determined that a large number of them are difficult for the BOP to manage and extremely challenging for the general prison population to get along with. Finally, the recent national witch-hunt against illegal immigration has generated a large number of uneducated prisoners, some of whom have extensive ties to gangs such as the Mara Salvatrucha (MS13), Aztecas and Border Brothers (Vaughan and Feere, 2008).

The foreign prisoners who fall into this category present special challenges for both staff and prisoners because the vast majority of them do not speak English and are associated with violent street gangs. Adding to this is the fact that most of these gangs are usually warring with one another and trying to keep up with who is beefing with who is an exercise in futility. Accordingly, these factors are largely responsible for the differences between the prisoners who were considered "the cream of the crop" and those of the new breed presently being warehoused by the BOP.

But what are some of the prison behaviours that are causing so much discontent among prisoners? Below I address three forms of prisoner behaviour that not only generate a great deal of complaining, but are also exacerbating the deterioration of relations with staff.

Prisoner Duplicity
Throughout the history of corrections COs and prisoners have engaged in a "cat and mouse" relationship. Prisoners have always tried to get away with as much as possible, while COs diligently worked to maintain some semblance of order. For the most part, both parties played by the rules and neither side pushed the other too far for fear of excessive retaliation. However, even within this Gordian convention prisoners of old carried themselves respectfully and understood the concept of "my word is my bond". In fact, the relationship between staff and prisoners was so well established that I can recall numerous occasions where staff turned to them to help resolve conflicts between rival gangs, among prisoners, and even between staff and prisoners. Unfortunately, today this is no longer the case.

Today, staff is cognizant that some members of this new generation of prisoners are all about 'rocking its enemy to sleep'. Officers realize that this recalcitrant group of individuals is only concerned about getting over on 'the man', regardless of the costs or consequences their actions may provoke the rest of the prison population by prison administrators. This fact is most evident in the number of privileges federal prisoners have lost over the last ten to fifteen years. For instance, at my present institution, FCC Coleman-Medium, commissary no longer sells hard candy, sugar or fresh fruits because these items are regularly used to cook wine. Additionally, prisoners and their families no longer have access to the outside visiting patio because of the selfish antics of a few prisoners who are more interested in five-minute thrills than the well-being of their peers. These little things may seem trivial, but for old prisoners that have spent decades behind bars and some who will never get out, they make all the difference in the world.

Indiscriminate Violence

Violence is embedded in prison life. And how can it not be? We throw together thousands of men from all walks of life and expect them to play nice. However, the violence I witnessed two decades ago was well-organized and motivated by the desire to correct a perceived wrong rather than by the act itself. Furthermore, old cons understood that violence was to be avoided because 1) it tends to escalate, especially between gangs, and 2) it only serves to "bring down more heat" on the rest of the prison population. Only the gravest of Code infractions merited the use of violence and then only after it had been sanctioned by the appropriate bodies.

In contrast, today's violence often lacks organization/structure, which means it is carried out haphazardly with little consideration as to how it will affect the rest of the prison population. Moreover, today's violence is perpetuated for the simple pleasure of the act itself. Taken together, this new twist on prison violence not only has undone what little respect staff once held for prisoners, but also has fostered a dog-eat-dog world where prisoners are more prone to resolve difference through violence than by parleying things out. This environment has led to greater distrust and hostility among prisoners and has contributed to the deterioration of staff/prisoner relations.

Sexual Misconduct

The introduction of female COs into the prison cellblocks has coincided with an epidemic of sexual misconduct. As more women have taken up what traditionally was considered a male posting, the number of prisoners receiving incident reports for stalking, indecent exposure, making sexual proposals, and sexual assault continues to be a challenge. Three interrelated causes account for this phenomenon.

First, I have noticed that the posting of female officers in housing units has increased the level of interaction between female staff and male prisoners. This protracted socialization has led to greater familiarization, which is not necessarily negative, but has provided more opportunities for sexual misconduct. Second, over the last several years the number of prisoners serving sentences for sexual offenses has nearly doubled, from 5,700 in May 2008 to 11,229 as of March 2013 (FBOP Quick Facts). Most of these prisoners, whose programming needs are arguably not met by authorities, seem to experience difficulty controlling their sexual urges, which makes them more prone to push the limits of what the BOP beholds as acceptable interaction between male prisoners and female staff members. Lastly, longer sentences means a larger number of prisoners have spent years (in some cases decades) without the companionship of the opposite sex. Some of these men are serving life sentences and are cognizant they will die in prison. Many of these prisoners feel they have little to lose by propositioning or, in some extreme cases, sexually assaulting a female staff member.

Hence, the collaboration of these causes appears to have increased the number of incident reports for sexual misconduct and also has deteriorated the symbiotic relationship that staff and old prisoners once enjoyed. Twenty years ago it was rare to hear that a prisoner was caught "gunning down" (the act of masturbating and/or exposing yourself) a female staff member. Today, this practice is very much en vogue, especially at the USP level. Unfortunately, this sort of behaviour not only creates a great deal of tension between staff and prisoners, but also generates a host of difficulties for the general prison population. For instance, a prisoner who keeps his hands inside his pant pockets for too long while in the presence of a female staff member is subject to be labelled a "gunner" and is dealt with accordingly.

In short, many younger federal prisoners tend to be deceptive, violent and disrespectful toward both staff and their fellow prisoners. Trying to talk sense to this new breed often feels like a waste of time. Therefore, it should come as no surprise that complaining about other prisoners is a major pastime for the majority of the BOP's prison population. However, the conundrum most prisoners fail to grasp is that the most vocal complainers are oblivious to the fact that they are the "other inmate" their peers complain about. In the end, complaining about other prisoners serves one vital function – it allows complainers to point their fingers at others for the prison conditions they themselves have helped create.

Solutions

The most efficacious solutions to prisoners' complaints are as simple as they are complex. Simple because prisoners have the wherewithal to change the prison conditions they complain about, and complex because, unfortunately, not enough of my peers are willing to accept responsibility for their past, present, and future behaviour, which is necessary to effect any meaningful change.

Accepting responsibility for our behaviour means acknowledging our contributions to the prison conditions we have helped create. It also means coming to terms with the fact that blaming external circumstances for our plight is a difficult business given the structural change in American society that is required. Scholars, prisoner authors, and well-meaning individuals can continue to point to all of the injustices committed by the criminal justice system, the flawed penology that led to the abandonment of the medical model of corrections, and whatever other social, economic, and political factors they deem responsible for the prison conditions we endure. However, these arguments have been vocalized over the last thirty years. And what has been accomplished? We presently have over 2.3 million men and women behind bars, at an estimated annual cost of over forty billion dollars (Ross, 2008, p. 61). We have approximately another five million individuals under some form of correctional control (Ross, 2013, p. 14). If these numbers do not awaken in us a sense of urgency regarding the conditions we find ourselves in, then I have no idea what will. So as I see it, we (prisoners) can either continue to wait for others to bring about the correctional and systematic changes they claim will liberate us from our miserable existence or we can take our lives and futures into our own hands. The bottom line is that no one is going to do for us what we are more than capable of doing for ourselves.

The first thing we must stop doing is passing on exaggerated versions of our criminal and correctional experiences. We need to understand that by embellishing our "war stories" and focusing on the worst of our prison experiences, we are perpetuating distorted images of who we (prisoners as a whole) really are. These warped images are used by the media, the entertainment industry, the government, and even some university professors to champion a malicious process known as "deviance amplification". Books such as Santos' *Inside: Life Behind Bars in America* and "reality" television shows like *Lockup* only serve to create what sociologists refer to as a "moral panic". Moral panics are used to manipulate the masses by corroborating the twisted images society already holds of a particular issue; in this case, of crime and corrections.

But this is not to say that bad things do not happen in prison – of course they do! However, what prison writers such as Bunker, Abbot and Santos have done is sensationalize the worst aspects of prison behaviour, which moral entrepreneurs use to justify their "tough on crime" posturing and policy making. In other words, some of our most popularized "storytelling" and our participation in skewed documentaries not only make the government's job easier but also facilitate the very prison conditions we complain about.

Second, we must make an individual and concerted stand against the tenets of the Convict Code. By succumbing to the Code's way of life and by allowing a small group of prisoners to dictate "what is" and "what is not" acceptable prison behaviour, we are not only fueling the prison conditions we complain about, but also guaranteeing for ourselves a round-trip ticket back to the penitentiary. We have to make it clear to this group of prisoners that we will not succumb to peer pressure, nor will we allow their threat of and/or use of violence to dictate our behaviour. Moreover, we must fight off the prison attitudes, habits, beliefs and expectations that have enslaved them to a life of misery. Indeed, we must simply refuse to become the hard-core, recidivist monsters they and the prison-industrial-complex wish to make of us.

Finally, we must stop blaming external circumstances for our predicaments. We are already cognizant that the Sentencing Reform Act of 1984 and other systematic factors have played significant roles in our lives. We have seen how these draconian laws have contributed to the deterioration of the federal prison system. However, with the exception of civil disobedience, we have no control over these juridical issues, nor do we have a say over the budgetary and staffing problems affecting the BOP. Therefore, why continue pointing to these issues as if by doing so they will magically disappear and our problems will go away? Instead, let us focus on what we can actually do to bring about the changes we desire.

Recidivism is the only factor of the correctional carrousel we have control over. And as demonstrated above, recidivism plays a significant role in the prison conditions we complain about. Hence, while incarcerated, we must do all we can to improve our odds of making a successful re-entry. How do we go about this? First, by accepting responsibility for our present and future well-being, and second by acquiring the social and job skills necessary to better our lives.

Throughout my incarceration, I have found that two factors account for most of the recidivists I have met: 1) the lack of employment opportunities for ex-prisoners and 2) the proliferation of substance abuse among my peers. Fortunately, the BOP offers numerous courses and programs aimed at helping prisoners develop the job skills they need and at assisting them overcome whatever addiction(s) they are struggling with.

Employability of Former-Prisoners

The fact that former prisoners have a more difficult time finding employment than the average citizen cannot be denied. In 2010, the Center for Economic and Policy Research conducted a study, which revealed "that a felony conviction or imprisonment significantly reduces the ability of ex-offenders to find jobs". Adding to this difficulty is the fact that prisoners are less educated, have less work experience, and lack social skills such as the ability to relate to people or be punctual (CEPR, 2010). All these factors contribute to the poor employability of former prisoners. However, I have found that with a little work and a steady dose of persistency these shortcomings can be overcome.

The foundation of a successful re-entry lies in our present willingness to make ourselves more attractive to employers upon release. This means that if a lack of education has been the weak link in your resume, then you must make your way to the education department and earn your General Equivalency Diploma (GED). If computers seem alien to you, get down to V. T. (Vocational Training) and take the Microsoft course. If your communication skills leave much to be desired, enrol in a public speaking class. In other words, take advantage of all the educational and vocational opportunities offered by the BOP.

In addition, through the BOP's Federal Prison Industry (UNICOR)[8] program, you can gain marketable job skills that can lead to viable and sustainable employment upon release (FBOP, 2012). I am aware the vast majority of prisoners do not want to participate in UNICOR, and that is unfortunate. Because even though UNICOR is a prison program that operates at a perennial financial loss and is known for its slave-labour wages,[9] research shows that those "inmates who work in UNICOR are twenty-four percent less likely to return to prison than their counterparts who did not participate in the UNICOR program" (Saylor and Gaes, 1997). These practical steps may seem insignificant, however, in the long run they may very well determine whether we make a successful re-entry or be counted as one more recidivist.

Overcoming Substance Abuse

Sixty percent of recidivists blame drug/alcohol abuse for their re-offending or violating supervised release (Pelissier *et al.*, 2000). But here again the

BOP offers several cognitive/behavioural programs that teach prisoners about "addiction" and provide practical tools to help them conquer their personal demons.

For example, the Residential Drug Abuse Program (RDAP) has been shown to lower both the rate of relapse and the rate of recidivism (Pelissier, 2000). RDAP is a 500-hours, unit-based program that keeps participants separated from the rest of the general prison population so that they can work together to create a community that supports pro-social attitudes and behaviours (BOP, Psychology Treatment Program, 2009). The aim of separating RDAP participants is so they can be kept away from the negative peer pressures of the larger prison environment (a.k.a. the ubiquitous Convict Code).

Other mental health treatment programs offered by the BOP include the Bureau Rehabilitation and Values Enhancement Program (BRAVE), the Skills Program, and the Axis II Program. These programs not only teach prisoners about the pitfalls of chemical dependency, but also challenge participants to examine their criminal thinking and antisocial behaviours.

Before closing this section, it is worth emphasizing that the success or failure of the above solutions is predicated on one simple but crucial element: a prisoner's readiness to accept responsibility for his or her past, present and future behaviour. Once this obstacle is overcome, I have found that then he or she can begin the painful, but rewarding, journey of "honestly [discovering] who he or she is and what he or she wants to be, and do the [necessary] work to accomplish the change" (Richards and Jones, p. 227). However, let us not kid ourselves. When all is said and done, it is not the programs we completed or the education and job skills we acquired while incarcerated that will determine our success or failure in the free world – albeit these things help – but rather the individual choices and decisions we make. In the end, we must all be cognizant that it all begins with us, and it all ends with us.

In sum, the solutions to our complaints are within our grasp. Unfortunately, I have noticed that too many of us lack the courage to speak out against the injustices we endure at the hands of our peers. For far too many of us, it is much easier to succumb to the Convict Code's way of life and to go along with prison rituals than to stand apart and face the wrath of all the foolishness around us. Sadly, this conduct is evident from the fact that seven out of ten of us find our way back to prison within three years of release.

Conclusion

Passing on exaggerated versions of our "war stories" and focusing on the worst of our prison behaviour is not going to improve the correctional conditions we complain about. On the contrary, these distorted images supply the ammunition moral entrepreneurs need to justify their "tough on crime" policy and legislation recommendations, which in turn exacerbate our present conditions and relegate us to second-class citizens upon our release. Our embellishments may provide the "effect" the literary world demands, and may even pad the wallets of those fortunate enough to have their work published. However, in the real world these colourful stories negatively "affect" the present and future survival of more than 2.3 million men and women behind bars.

In addition, wasting our time in front of idiot boxes and complaining about juridical issues beyond our control is asinine. If we want to effect changes within the Federal Bureau of Prisons, then we must stop waiting on others to do for us what only we can do for ourselves. By bettering ourselves we will not only improve our odds of making a successful re-entry, but also do our part to ease the prison conditions we complain so much about.

Finally, I want to address those prisoners who so willingly succumb to the Convict Code's way of life and so readily adopt the prison attitudes, habits, beliefs, and expectations that practically guarantee your return trip to the penitentiary. I know how difficult it is to stand apart from all the nonsense we endure on a daily basis. But despite these challenges, I encourage you to do so.

ENDNOTES

*   I would like to thank the following individuals. My parents, Margarita and Rolando Zaldivar, for believing in me even when I did not believe in myself. My children, Michelle, Priscilla and Michael Zaldivar, for their generous assistance and input; Michi, I could not have done it without your help. Dr. Justin Piché for this invaluable opportunity and support throughout the writing process, as well as the anonymous reviewers for their time, comments and suggestions, and their willingness to work with me. Your comments fuelled my desire to see this project through. The prisoners at FCC Coleman USP1, MEDIUM, and LOW are also acknowledged for putting up with my ceaseless prodding and probing. I hope I remained loyal to your views. And last, but by no means least, I would like to express my deepest gratitude to Dr. Jeffrey Ian Ross. Professor, this paper is as much yours as it is mine. I thank you for all the time, patience, guidance, teachings, and understanding you have provided throughout the years. I am forever in your debt.

[1] Throughout this paper I use the term "prisoner" rather than "inmate". I do this out of consideration for the work of the men and women who make up the *Journal of Prisoners on Prisons* and the school of Convict Criminology. I also refrain as much as possible from using the term "convict" because regardless of the contentions of some Convict Criminologists (See Richards, 2005, p. 193), I believe the term, as defined by Charles Huckelbury (2009, pp. 24-25), breeds a mindset that causes more harm than benefit in the lives of more than 2.3 million men and women behind bars.

[2] The Convict Code is a set of rules by which prisoners live. For example, prisoners are to mind their own business, have access to a weapon at all times, stab rats, and kill child molesters, look out for homeboys, stay away from punks (homosexuals), and are absolutely not to socialize with staff.

[3] In 2002, I was awarded a Bachelor of Science in Business Administration from Saint Mary College (Leavenworth, Kansas) and in 2008 a Bachelor of Science in Sociology/Criminology from Colorado State University (Pueblo, Colorado).

[4] Recidivism is here defined as "re-incarceration", regardless of whether it is due to re-offending and/or violating conditions of supervised release. It is also noted that the term "recidivism" is a "complex phenomenon that is difficult to define and measure" (Ross, 2008, p. 140). It is further acknowledged that "Most men and women who go back to prison do so for [probation and] parole violations" (Ross and Richards, 2009, p. xi). Still, none of these factors alter the dynamics of the overcrowding riddle. Whether we (prisoners) return to prison for new crimes or probation and/or parole violations does not change the fact there are simply too many of us behind bars.

[5] Personal conversations with staff members at FCC Coleman-Medium. The names of officers have been omitted at their request.

[6] See endnote 5.

[7] A fictitious name created to facilitate the writing/reading process.

[8] The BOP's Federal Prison Industries, Incorporated (FPI), better known as UNICOR, is a wholly-owned government corporation. UNICOR was created, in part, by President Franklin D. Roosevelt's Executive Order 6917, issued on December 11, 1934. (BOP, Factories with Fences, 2012)

[9] Working in UNICOR earns a prisoner between $.23 to $1.65 per hour depending on pay grade and longevity.

REFERENCES

Allen, Harry F., Clifford E. Simonsen and Edward J. Latessa (2004) *Corrections in America: An Introduction,* Upper Saddle River (NJ): Pearson Prentice Hall.

Beck, Allen J. and Shipley, Bernard E. (1989) *Recidivism of Prisoners Released in 1983,* Bureau of Justice Statistics, U.S. Department of Justice. NCJ-116261.

Brown, Stephen E., Finn-Aage Esbensen, and Gilbert Geis (2004*) Criminology: Explaining crime and its context (5th ed.). Study Guide*, Cincinnati (OH): Anderson Publishing Co.

Center for Economic and Policy Research (2010) Ex-Offenders and the Labor Market –
    November. Retrieved from www.thegrio.com.
Cooper v. Oklahoma [1996] 517 U.S. 348.
Ehrlich, Susan A. (2000) "The Increasing Federalization of Crime", *Arizona State Law
    Journal, 825*: 825 – 841.
Fathi, David (2011) "Custody vs. Treatment Debate. Addicted to Punishment", *National
    Liberator*, 15(3): 12.
Federal Bureau of Prisons (2012) "Factories with Fences", Federal Bureau of Prisons
    Office of Research and Evaluation – March.
Federal Bureau of Prisons (no date), *Quick Facts About the Bureau of Prisons.* Retrieved
    from www.bop.gov/news/quick.jsp.
Langan, Patrick A. and David J. Levine (2002) *Recidivism of Prisoners Released in
    1994*, Bureau of Justice Statistics, U. S. Department of Justice, NCJ 193427.
Huckelbury, Charles (2009) "Talking Points: How Language Functions as a Status
    Determinant in Prison", *Journal of Prisoners on Prisons,* 18(1&2): 22-28.
Pelissier, Bernadette, William Rhodes, Wiliam Saylor, Gerry Gaes, Scott D. Camp, Suzy
    D. Vanyur, and Sue Wallace (2000) "TRAID Drug Treatment Evaluation Project",
    Final Report of Three-Year Outcomes Federal Bureau of Prisons Office of Research
    and Evaluation.
Richards, Stephen C. (2005) "Born Illegal", *Storytelling Sociology: Narrative as Social
    Inquiry*, in Ronald J. Berger and Richard Quinney (eds.), Colorado: Lynne Rienner
    Inc., pp.183-193.
Richards, Stephen C. and Richard S. Jones (2004) "Beating the Perpetual Incarceration
    Machine: Overcoming Structural Impediments to Re-entry", in Shadd Maruna
    and Russ Immarigeon (eds.), *After Crime and Punishment: Pathway to Offender
    Reintegration* Cullompton, Devon: Willan Publishing, pp. 201-232.
Ross, Jeffrey Ian (2013) "Invention of the American Supermax Prison", in Jeffrey Ian
    Ross (ed.), *The Globalization of Supermax Prisons,* New Jersey: Rutgers University
    Press, pp. 10-24.
Ross, Jeffrey Ian (2008) *Special Problems in Corrections*, Upper Saddle River, New
    Jersey: Pearson Education Inc.
Ross, Jeffrey Ian and Richards C. Richards (2009) *Beyond Bars: Rejoining society after
    prison*, Alpha Books, New York (NY): Penguin Group Inc.
Saylor, William G. and Gerald G. Gaes (1997) "Post Release Employment Project",
    Correctional Management Quarterly, 1(2).
Sykes, Gresham M. (1958) *The Society of Captives: A Study of a Maximum Security
    Prison*, Princeton University Press: Princeton Paperback, 1971.
The Sentencing Project (no date) *The Federal Prison Population: A Statistical Analysis.*,
    retrieved from www.sentencingproject.org.
U. S. Department of Justice (2009) Federal Bureau of Prisons, *Psychology Treatment
    +Program. P5330.11* Washington (DC): BOP.
Vaughan, Jessica M. and Jon D. Feere (2008) "Taking Back the Streets: ICE and Local
    Law Enforcement Target Immigrant Gangs", Center for Immigration Studies,
    Washington, DC (www.cis.org).
Washington Post (2006) "Lorton, From Prison to Parkland" – March. Retrieved from http://
    www.washingtonpost.com/wpdyn/content/article/2006/03/22/AR2006032200860.html.

ABOUT THE AUTHOR

Miguel Zaldivar is a first-time, nonviolent prisoner in his twenty-fourth year of a thirty- year sentence for drug related crimes. While incarcerated, Zaldivar has earned baccalaureate degrees in Business Administration and Sociology/Criminology. He has also completed over fifty cognitive/ behavioural programs and educational courses. For the last decade, he has served as a Suicide Companion. From 2002 to 2006, he was a spokesperson for FCC Coleman USP1's Community Outreach Program. He is currently at Federal Correctional Complex Coleman Low.

RESPONSE

Reflecting on 25 Years of the *Journal of Prisoners on Prisons*
Bob Gaucher

INTRODUCTION

The *Journal of Prisoners on Prisons* (JPP) follows the tradition of the North American penal press by focusing on prison life and the issues that are at the forefront of prisoners' concerns. The heyday of the penal press was from the 1930s to the 1960s in the United States, and from 1950 through the 1980s in Canada. Its emergence reflects the raison d'être of penal authorities to reform the silent system prison regimes that were in place and move towards the creation of "rehabilitative" correctional institutions. This transformation required the freeing up of prisoners' movements and activities, as a necessary precursor to the functioning of rehabilitative programs, which was evident in the creation of the penal press. Authorities in both jurisdictions supported the penal press as a means to garner backing for prison reform from politicians and the general public within the containing civil societies.

This is clearly the case in Canada, where the penal press was encouraged and supported by the new (post-Second World War) Commissioner's Office as a means of selling penal reform to the general public and to prisoners. The *Kingston Penitentiary Telescope* – which commenced publication on September 1, 1950 – was the first Canadian penal press magazine, becoming a flagship for penal reform. The positive reception of *the KP Telescope* is evidenced by its success; by 1954 it had over 4,000 outside subscribers and was available to prisoners in all federal penitentiaries. *Pen-O-Rama* – established in 1950 and produced by prisoners in St. Vincent de Paul Penitentiary (Montréal) – had numerous advertisers, including Coca-Cola and the Hudson Bay Company.[1]

There have been over 150 penal press magazines published from federal penitentiaries in Canada, as well as an array of others from provincial prisons and reformatories. Like the early years of the *KP Telescope,* some of these publications have influenced Canadian penal policy and civil society. For example, this is the case for the penal reform initiatives of the 1950s, and during the period of heightened prisoners' resistance in the 1970s and 1980s, as exemplified in the creation and spread of *Prison Justice Day* (PJD). This day was conceived and created by prisoners in Millhaven Penitentiary as a response to the constant threats and aggressive actions of out of control prison staff following the premature opening of this super-maximum penitentiary in the 1970s. Long-term prisoners there established the *Quarter Century Group*, which later became the *Odyssey Group*, and conceived of *PJD* as a means of engaging prisoners and the general public in a discussion about the violent repression perpetrated by prison guards across the federal penitentiary system in Canada at that time (see McNeil and Vance, 1976; Culhane, 1979). With the assistance of the editors of *Tightwire* – published by prisoners at Kingston Prison for Women – and social justice activists like Claire Culhane and Liz Elliott, *PJD* spread countrywide and came to be observed annually on August 10th in all federal penal institutions, and in ceremonies held in numerous Canadian cities (Gaucher, 1990-91). The Canadian penal press played a major role in establishing its national scope.

What distinguishes the *JPP* is the academic nature of the publication, the first and only such scholarly journal. The project is a university-based, peer-reviewed journal that follows the general format of traditional social science publications. It publishes the analysis and commentary of prisoners, former prisoners, and prisoners' families on criminal justice and penal justice issues. The original intent of the *JPP* was "to bring the knowledge and experience of the incarcerated to bear upon […] academic arguments and concerns and to inform public discourse about the current state of our carceral institutions" (Gaucher, 1988, p. 54). Our motto – "allowing our experiences and analysis to be added to the forum that will constitute public opinion could help to halt the disastrous trend toward building more fortresses of fear which will become in the 21st century this generation's monuments to failure" – conceived for the first issue by Jo-Ann Mayhew (1988), captures the essence of our intent.

The *JPP* is an academic journal that uniquely provides the insider knowledge and analysis of a major player in prison life and the primary commodity of the prison industrial complex, the prisoner. It aims to address a lacuna in penology and criminology, by adding the voices and understandings of prisoners to our academic and political scrutiny of penal custom internationally (Piché, Gaucher and Walby, forthcoming). In my *Response* to the first issue (Gaucher, 1988) I noted the influence that prisoners had on the creation of the new critical criminology that emerged in the 1970s. This was represented in the United Kingdom in the seminal work of Stanley Cohen and Laurie Taylor (1972), *Psychological Survival: the Experience of Long-Term Imprisonment,* which arose out of the authors' teaching a university course to prisoners in a high-security prison and the influence generally of prisoners on the new criminologists in that country.[2] In the United States, the radical analysis of Tony Platt, Paul Takagi and the Berkeley Center for Research On Criminal Justice was highly influenced by prisoners (Gaucher, 1988). By the mid-1980s this influence on academic discourse had obviously waned. The *JPP* was in part, a response to prisoners slipping back into the shadows and out of academic consciousness.[3]

ORIGINS

The *JPP* was conceived and created within the nexus of the International Conference on Penal Abolition (ICOPA), a grassroots movement focused on overturning the dominant punitive response of criminal justice and penal servitude to ongoing social conflict and inequality. In the current acceptance of expanding definitions of crime and the wholesale incarceration of marginalized and disenfranchised populations, ICOPA's mandate to reduce and abolish carceral solutions appears to be truly "radical". However, when ICOPA held its first congress in Toronto in 1983, there was still a lingering hope that the liberalization of criminal justice policy and a reduction in penal populations could be achieved by a move towards community-based solutions to social conflict such as reconciliation, approaches that are now regrouped under the restorative justice banner, decriminalization and decarceration. Indeed, as first conceived ICOPA was a response to the punitive shift to the right and cutbacks of the welfare state that was emerging in the Thatcher, Reagan, and Mulroney era of neo-conservative politics and get tough on crime ideology. We still had hope for a new tomorrow.

ICOPA I (Toronto) – although it included academic contributors, like Norwegian Thomas Mathiesen[4] – was largely a grassroots initiative, and prominently featured Canadian activists such as Claire Culhane,[5] Art Solomon[6] and Ruth Morris.[7] ICOPA II (1985) was held Amsterdam, Netherlands, and provided a greater academic contextualization and legitimation of our arguments . This congress led to the reformulation of the mandate from a primary focus on "prison abolition" to the broader focus, relocating the analysis of the prison within the complex social structures, social relations and social control institutions of western societies; that is, "penal" abolition.[8]

That congress was not without controversy. The organizers, principally René Van Swaanigen, who represented the emerging counter-intuitive school of "realist criminology", brought the academic contest of abolitionism versus realist positions in critical criminology to the fore.[9] He seemed to have concluded that "ICOPA liberals" were in need of a reality check. On the second day of the congress, during the lunch break, the staged theft of a woman's purse erupted in the university cafeteria where delegates were gathered. At a table of Canadian activists (Claire Culhane, Art Solomon, Liz Elliott and Howard Davidson) with whom I sat, the "set up" was obvious. The arrest of the perpetrator shortly after the event was a further indication to our group that this event was not real. This was not the case for many other (liberal?) delegates who were immediately concerned. When we arrived for the post-lunch plenary session, we discovered that it had been cancelled and replaced by a pre-written lecture on criminal victimization by a local police psychologist. The cat was out of the bag! During the ensuing uproar, a number of us left and went outside for a smoke and discussed this childish and insulting turn of events. It encouraged us to turn a discriminating eye on the congress and the direction our movement seemed to be headed. While many of the European academics were enriching our intellectual grasp and analysis of the issues, we worried about the absence of grassroots involvement and the paucity of prisoners' voices at this congress. This directed us, with the support of some activists and academics from the United States, to ensure that ICOPA III would return to our home soil. It was agreed that the next congress would be held in Canada. ICOPA III was hosted by the Université de Montréal in 1987.

As an organizer of the English language sessions at that congress, I made a major effort to invite and include grassroots activists and organizations, with a particular emphasis on First Nations involvement.[10] The Native Women's Association of Canada and Patricia Monture[11] made presentations, and Lew Gurwitz brought a large delegation from the Leonard Peltier Defense Committee.[12] The Toronto-based *Anarchist Black Cross- Rainbow Coalition* and their associated group, *Radical Fairies,* played an important part at the congress. We were particularly keen to have prisoners' presentations, although getting prisoners out to attend a penal abolition conference was obviously problematic. In a session organized by Professor Barker (Boston College) on prison education, Howard Davidson and I presented papers written by Canadian prisoners with whom we were working at that time.[13]

The session was very well received and it encouraged a discussion amongst Canadian activists as to how we could increase the involvement of prisoners at ICOPA, more generally within the abolition movement, and in academic discourse. The result was the creation of the *JPP.* The original editorial board was drawn from these discussions, with Howard Davidson acting as editor. Our thinking was informed by the (then) recent success of the Canadian penal press, especially *Odyssey* (Millhaven), *Tightwire* (Kingston Prison for Women) and *Tarpaper* (Matsqui) in establishing *PJD* observance in Canada. With people like Claire Culhane and Liz Elliott in our group discussions, we came to the conclusion that a journal that was published outside, beyond the control of prison censorship, made sense and offered prisoners a real possibility to engage the society that caged them. As we conceived it, the prisoner would not be a mere ethnographic subject, but the ethnographer of the prisons and societies they lived in (Gaucher, 1988).

25ᵀᴴ ANNIVERSARY OF PUBLICATION

I find it difficult to get my head around the fact that the *JPP* has been publishing prisoners' writing for 25 years. Over those many years I have been privileged to work with creative, inquiring and committed people who have provided the articles, and managed the editing and production. We have been particularly fortunate to have had contributions from outstanding prisoner activists and writers from Canada, the United States, Ireland, Australia, South America and elsewhere. The many outstanding artists whose work has graced the covers of the publications added immeasurably to the quality of the Journal.[14]

The creation and first publication of the *JPP* in 1988 took place in the context of the rapid expansion of prisons across western democratic societies, led by the carceral binge occurring in the United States. While successive liberal governments in Canada engaged in prison construction, the hard turn towards retributive criminal justice policy and a consequent explosion of prison populations that took place in the United States did not occur here. The freedom of prisoners to engage in academic and public discourse is indicative of the policy direction of governments. As previously noted, when the Canadian and American states embarked on the policy of penal reform, the penal press and the voices of prisoners were utilized as a means of encouraging public support for rehabilitative as opposed to strictly punitive penal regimes. In the United States, the "get tough on crime" political mantra of the 1980s, and subsequent rejection of the rehabilitative model, led to the return to punitive warehousing regimes and the massive expansion of penal institutions and prison populations. The accompanying silencing of prisoners was a consequent of New York State style "Son of Sam" legislation, purported to prevent criminals from financially benefiting from their writing about their crimes,[15] along with the proliferation of Marion style closed/locked down prisons that greatly curtailed prisoners' access to the outside (Morgan and Reed, 1993).

Despite the increasing recognition of the problematic nature and obvious failure of this approach in the United States, the current reactionary Canadian Conservative government is attempting to reproduce this model of repression in Canada. As the Reform Party, they endorsed the "get tough on crime" political gambit which included an attempt to silence prison writers via Bill C-205/220 (1997), which aimed at preventing prisoners from publishing their writing.[16] After their takeover of the Conservative Party of Canada and their ascension to power, this government has made major punitive changes to law and prison regimes. These changes include an array of mandatory sentences that abrogate judicial discretion and delimit the possibility of community-based sentences and supervised parole. The growth in prison populations these changes promote are being realized.[17] These changes have been accompanied by the demise of lower security institutions (Farm Camps), as well as the curtailment of access to prisons by family, visitors and prison-focused groups. This delimiting of public access and the ability to scrutinize the operation of prisons deems the continuation of publications such as the *JPP* as important as ever in Canada.

Over the past 25 years this Journal has encouraged prisoners to write of their experience of criminalization and penal servitude, to analyze that experience and to reclaim their own humanity in the process. A number of our contributors gained confidence in their writing and their ability to engage the outside world through publication in the *JPP*, which led to their success in publishing books and articles in mainstream magazines and newspapers.[18] Our writers' articles have influenced thousands of university students, helping them to overcome dominant stereotypes and fictional representations of crime and criminality (Gaucher, 1986). Discovering that prisoners can eloquently and analytically engage the subject of their studies has helped many students understand the contradiction between popular images of crime and criminal justice and the academic critique of *criminal just-us*. Prisoners' analyses serve to ground this critique in the flesh, blood and torment of real human beings.

I have worked with prisoners on this Journal since its inception and been rewarded for doing so in numerous ways. The lasting friendships stand out. The contributions of our writers, especially those whose work sustained the Journal over many years, established the *JPP* as a unique and important entity within academic criminology. Our contributors taught me, and kept me informed of changes and the impact of legislation. This was the case from my initial engagements (see Jo-Ann Mayhew (1988)) and continues to this day. Imprisonment is a high-risk engagement and a number of these friends have died in prison. I was devastated by the murder of James Allridge III by the State of Texas on August 26, 2004 (Gaucher, 2005) and overwhelmed by the news of Victor Hassine's death (Gaucher, 2008). For many years I worked closely with Little Rock Reed and his sudden accidental death shortly after being released left so much promise unrealized. The *JPP* belongs to all of our contributors. I know that I speak for all of us who have worked on the outside when I say thanks for taking us along.

A quarter-century of publication would not have been possible without the efforts and hard work of the many people who have worked on the outside to ensure its continued existence. Unpaid and largely unrecognized, they have worked diligently to ensure that we have a high quality journal that meets the academic and aesthetic standards of the writers and artists we have featured. Without their commitment the *JPP* would have expired years ago. The spirit of Claire Culhane, and the friendship and many contributions of Liz Elliott, inspired this Journal from its inception. 25 years of publication attests to their success.

ENDNOTES

[1] See Gaucher (1989). Many of these Canadian penal press magazines may be accessed at <www.penalpress.com>.
[2] See Taylor, Walton and Young (1973; 1975).
[3] This is exemplified in an article by Ratner and Cartwright (1990), which was debated in the *JPP* (see Ratner, 1993; Gaucher, 1993).
[4] See Mathiesen (1974) which is a seminal text for the penal abolition movement. Professor Mathiesen addressed the first ICOPA held in Toronto in 1983.
[5] See Culhane (1985) and Lowe (1992). Claire addressed the first ICOPA held in Toronto in 1983.

6   Arthur Solomon, an Anishnawbe Elder, worked closely with Aboriginal prisoners in Canada to establish spiritual rights for First Nations prisoners. He was instrumental in creating the *Canadian Association in Support of Native People* (Toronto), a group who were actively involved in a wide variety of issues affecting native people, including imprisonment (see Solomon 1990a; Solomon, 1990b). Art addressed the first ICOPA held in Toronto in 1983 and was a participant in subsequent ICOPAs .

7   Ruth Morris was a creator of ICOPA and until her death in 2000 was instrumental in co-ordinating the bi-annual congresses across the world. Ruth championed alternative approaches to punitive criminal justice such as reconciliation, restorative and transformative justice (see Morris, 1995; Morris, 2000).

8   Conference organizers published a text of papers from this congress (see Bianchi and van Swaaningen, 1986). Stan Cohen (1986) also edited an issue of *Contemporary Crises: Law, Crime and Social Change,* focused upon the discourse on "abolitionism" at this congress.

9   A presentation by Louk Hulsman "Critical Criminology and the Concept of Crime" critiqued "realist criminology" and became a bedrock argument of the penal abolition movement. Fittingly, it was published in both the post-congress texts noted above (see supra note 8).

10 First Nations peoples are vastly overrepresented in Canadian prisons.

11 A Mohawk woman, Trish started to work with Arthur Solomon and Aboriginal prisoners in Kingston (Canada) area penitentiaries while a law student at Queen's University (see Monture-Angus, 1995).

12 Lew Gurwitz of the Leonard Peltier Defense Committee of Kansas and Frank Dreaver of its Toronto counterpart made presentations at ICOPA and a number of other events in Montréal. In 1987, they helped co-ordinate a major initiative around Bill M-28 in Canada's federal parliament in Ottawa, which aimed to have Leonard released from custody and returned to Canada because of the illegality of his extradition to the United States. Arthur Solomon and the *Canadian Association in Support of Native People* were involved in both of these initiatives.

13 The first volume of the *JPP* featured these articles.

14 The most notable of the many outstanding contributors was Norval Morrisseau, the Ojibway "shaman artist". Our first coloured cover, featuring his work, sold out immediately, in no small measure due to his fame in Canada.

15 New York State Executive Law 632-a, 1977, was subsequently amended, challenged and copied by other States throughout the 1980s.

16 For a full discussion of this censorship initiative see Gaucher and Elliott (2001). This Private Members Bill was maneuvered through the House of Commons by shifting the focus away from the wealth of evidence that would undermine its passage and masking the ramifications of its enactment with the rhetoric of moral indignation and stated concern for victims of crime, which characterize the Reform Party / Conservative Party duplicity on criminal justice issues. The thorough scrutiny this Bill received during Senate Hearings led to its rejection. At that time, Curtis Taylor and I distributed copies of the *JPP* (1997, 8:1-2) to all members of the Senate Committee, and Stephen Reed as a representative of PEN (Poets, Playwrights, Editors, Essayists, and Novelists) and the *JPP* addressed the Hearings.

17   For a discussion of recent developments, consult the blog posts written by Justin
     Piché at <www.tpcp-canada.blogspot.ca>.
18   For example see Little Rock Reed (1993), Victor Hassine (1996, 2005), and Charles
     Huckelbury (2008).

REFERENCES

Bianchi, Herman and René van Swaaningen (eds.) (1986) *Abolitionism: Towards a Non-Repressive Approach to Crime*, Amsterdam: Free University Press.

Cohen, Stan (ed.) (1986) *Contemporary Crises: Law, Crime and Social Change*, 10(1), Martinus Nijhoff Publishers.

Cohen, Stanley and Laurie Taylor (1972) *Psychological Survival: The Experience of Long-term Imprisonment*, London: Penguin Books.

Culhane, Claire (1985) *Still Barred from Prison: Social Injustice in Canada*, Montréal: Black Rose Books.

Culhane, Claire (1979) *Barred From Prison: A Personal Account*, Vancouver: Pulp Press.

Gaucher, Bob (2008) "Dedication for Victor Hassine", *Journal of Prisoners on Prisons*, 17(1): 1-3.

Gaucher, Bob (2005) "Victims – Both Sides: A Tribute to James V. Allridge III (1962-2004)", *Journal of Prisoners on Prisons*, 14(1): 101-107.

Gaucher, Bob (1993) "Too Many Chiefs", *Journal of Prisoners on Prisons*, 4(2): 135-139.

Gaucher, Bob (1990-1991) "Organizing Inside: Prison Justice Day (August 10th) A Non-Violent Response To Penal Repression", *Journal of Prisoners on Prisons*, 3(1-2): 93-110.

Gaucher, Bob (1989) "The Canadian Penal Press: A Documentation and Analysis", *Journal of Prisoners on Prisons*, 2(1): 3-24.

Gaucher, Bob (1988) "The Prisoner As Ethnographer: The Journal of Prisoners on Prisons", *Journal of Prisoners on Prisons*, 1(1): 49-62.

Gaucher, Bob (1986) "Teaching Criminology: Crime News and Crime Fiction — Offsetting the Influence of the Mass Media", in Herman Bianchi and René van Swaaningen (eds.), *Abolitionism: Towards a Non-Repressive Approach to Crime*, Amsterdam: Free University Press, pp. 61-69.

Gaucher, Bob and Liz Elliott (2001) "*Sister of Sam*: The Rise and Fall of Bill C-205/220", *The Windsor Yearbook of Access To Justice*, 72-105.

Hassine, Victor (1996) *Life Without Parole: Living in Prison Today*, Los Angeles: Roxbury Publishing.

Hassine, Victor, Robert Johnson and Ania Dobrzanska (2005) *The Crying Wall and Other Prison stories*, West Conshohocken; Infinity Publishing Company.

Huckelbury, Charles (2008) *Tales From The Purple Penguin*, Henniker (NH): BleakHouse Publishing

Hulsman, Louk (1986) "Critical Criminology and the Concept of Crime", *Abolitionism: Towards a Non-repressive Approach to Crime*, 10(1): 25-41.

Lowe, Mick (1992) *One Woman Army: the Life of Claire Culhane*, Toronto: Macmillan Canada.

Mathiesen, Thomas (1974) *The Politics of Abolition*, London: Martin Robinson & Company.

Mayhew, Jo-Anne (1988) "Corrections is A Male Enterprise", *Journal of Prisoners on Prisons,* 1(1): 11-21.

McNeil, Gerard with Sharon Vance (1978) *Cruel and Unusual*, Canada: Deneau and Greenberg.

Monture-Angus, Patricia (1995) *Thunder in My Soul: A Mohawk Woman Speaks*, Toronto: Fernwood Publishing.

Morgan, Lisa and Little Rock Reed (eds.) (1993) *Journal of Prisoners on Prisons*, 4(2).

Morris, Ruth (2000) *Stories of Transformative Justice*, Toronto: Canadian Scholar's Press.

Morris, Ruth (1995) *Penal Abolition: The Practical Choice,* Toronto: Canadian Scholar's Press.

Piché, Justin, Bob Gaucher and Kevin Walby (forthcoming) "Facilitating Prisoner Ethnography: An Alternative Approach to 'Doing Prison Research Differently'", *Qualitative Inquiry.*

Ratner, Robert S. and Barry Cartwright (1990) "Politicized Prisoners: From Class Warriors to Faded Rhetoric", *Journal of Human Justice*, 2(1): 75-92.

Ratner, Robert S. (1993) "A Reply To Robert Gaucher", *Journal of Prisoners on Prisons*, 4(2): 133-34.

Reed, Little Rock (ed.) (1993) *The American Indian in the White Man's Prisons: A Story of Genocide*, Taos (NM): Uncompromising Books.

Solomon, Arthur (1994) *Eating Bitterness: A Vision Beyond The Prison Walls*, (Cathleen Kneen and Michael Posluns, Editors), Toronto: NC Press.

Solomon, Arthur, (1990a) "If There is No Justice There is No Peace", *Journal of Prisoners on Prisons*, 2(2): 29-38.

Solomon, Arthur (1990b) *Songs For The People: Teachings On The Natural Way*, (Michael Posluns, Editor), Toronto: NC Press.

Taylor, Ian, Paul Walton and Jock Young (eds.) (1975) *Critical Criminology*, London: Routledge & Kegan Paul Ltd.

Taylor, Ian, Paul Walton and Jock Young (1973) *The New Criminology: For a Social Theory of Deviance*, London: Routledge & Kegan Paul Ltd.

ABOUT THE AUTHOR

Bob Gaucher is a retired faculty member from the Department of Criminology at the University of Ottawa. He is currently Editor-in-Chief of the *JPP* and is one of the founding members of the publication's Editorial Board.

PRISONERS' STRUGGLES

Quand une chorégraphe rencontre une criminologue : Parcours insolite
Claire Jenny et Sylvie Frigon

L a danse en prison ? Deux termes en opposition ? La démarche évoquée dans cet article est née d'une rencontre entre deux mondes, deux univers, deux disciplines et deux personnes : *Claire Jenny*, danseuse et chorégraphe de la compagnie Point Virgule à Paris, et, *Sylvie Frigon*, professeure titulaire au Département de criminologie et titulaire de la Chaire de recherche « La prison dans la culture, la culture dans la prison » à la Faculté des sciences sociales de l'Université d'Ottawa.

Dans cet article sous forme de discussion, nous présentons : 1) la compagnie de danse contemporaine française Point Virgule ; 2) la fondamentaux de la danse ; 3) le corps incarcéré et la danse ; et 4) les projets menés en milieu universitaire.

LA COMPAGNIE DE DANSE CONTEMPORAINE FRANÇAISE POINT VIRGULE
* Photographe de Claire Jenny, chorégraphe

En 1999, *Claire Jenny* créée sa première pièce Jeune public Touche à Tout. Très vite reconnue par un large réseau de scènes dédiées à l'enfance, elle met en œuvre Prendre l'air en 2006, *Incertain corps* en 2008 et *Le corps en délibéré* en 2009. L'ensemble de ces créations destinées aux tous petits l'a longuement mené sur les routes de France au cours d'importantes tournées, 360 représentations à ce jour.

Personne Ressource pour la danse à l'école en France, *Claire Jenny* mène de nombreux projets reliant ses processus artistiques et les enjeux de l'éducation de l'enfant. Elle définit sa démarche par un questionnement : « *qu'est-ce qui fait qu'on tient debout, en équilibre et en interaction*

paisible avec notre environnement ? ». Quelques soient les contextes de ses projets (des prisons en passant par les cités des banlieues françaises jusqu'aux territoires palestiniens), elle déploie un cheminement sensible sur le devenir de l'humain, sur l'humain en devenir, sur ses qualités de présence (estime de soi et accueil de l'autre) et ses capacités à absorber, à rebondir, à se transformer.

De 1995 à 2006, elle mène une douzaine de projets de créations en milieu carcéral mêlant personnes détenues et artistes de la compagnie Point Virgule en France et au Québec. Cette démarche encore trop rare car elle questionne sensiblement les enjeux de l'enfermement des corps a été soutenue par le Ministère de la culture et de la communication français dans le cadre d'une « aide à la recherche et à l'écriture », par la Fondation Beaumarchais et par l'AFAA – ex Institut français– dans le cadre du programme « En quête d'auteurs ». À Montréal elle fût accueillie par La Fondation Jean-Pierre Perreault et la Saison Danse Danse. En 2009, elle publie « Chairs incarcérées : une exploration de la danse en prison », ouvrage coécrit avec Sylvie FRIGON, professeure au Département de criminologie à l'Université d'Ottawa. Bouleversée par ces rencontres artistiques et humaines singulières, *Claire Jenny* créée deux pièces en écho à cette expérience : *Résilience* en 2001 (un hommage aux moments intenses partagés avec les détenues de la Maison d'arrêt des femmes de Fresnes au cours des différentes interventions de la compagnie depuis 1996) et en 2004 *Cheminement* (un solo dansé qui prend sa source dans ce qui nous fonde, ce qui nous permet de rester en équilibre).

Aujourd'hui, à la lisière de l'ensemble de ces expériences, nourries par elle, *Claire Jenny* crée *Chairs (de) femmes* en 2010 et *Éffigies* en 2011; deux projets de créations pour explorer la modélisation des représentations féminines et la manière dont elle détermine nos pratiques, nos manières d'être et de paraître, notre vision.

> Actuellement, je diffuse les fondamentaux de ma démarche artistique dans tous les contextes : les pièces que je crée, les ateliers de pratique avec les amateurs et les différents temps de rencontres avec les publics (répétitions publiques, conférences, débats,…). Et quelques soient les situations, je suis portée par la transmission des œuvres, de la saveur, des valeurs, de la pensée, de la pratique de l'art de la danse.
>
> – Claire Jenny

LES FONDAMENTAUX DE LA DANSE

Tout au long du XXe siècle et encore aujourd'hui, les grands créateurs de la danse contemporaine n'ont pas assujetti leur art à des normes ou à des modèles, même si des courants de pensée et de pratique chorégraphiques ont réuni des artistes à certaines époques et en certains lieux. Cet art élabore des notions singulières de l'humain en sollicitant des sensations, des actes, des attitudes et des représentations du corps – ses mises en jeu dans le mouvement, les rapports qu'il entretient avec l'espace, les manières dont il se positionne dans le temps, les modes relationnels qu'il investit. Par le questionnement perpétuel sous-tendant les démarches de création, par les sujets abordés et les manières de concevoir et de présenter les spectacles, cet art ne cesse de se transformer. Danser, c'est appréhender l'autre, le monde avec « le mouvement du corps [...] comme instrument de savoir, de pensée, et d'expression » (Louppe, 1997, p. 61). La danse contemporaine met en scène « un corps d'abîme » (ibid, p. 46), poreux, lieu de passage entre soi et le monde, lieu de dépôt de nos perceptions qui fonde le sens d'une œuvre chorégraphique.

La danse met en jeu l'être dans sa globalité. Elle sollicite et interroge le sens de l'existence. Elle nous renseigne sur les trajets de nos vies. Le mouvement dansé imprègne celui qui l'exécute tout comme celui qui l'accueille, dans un échange intime de perceptions; le sens de la danse se situe quelque part entre ce que proposent le chorégraphe auteur et les danseurs interprètes, et ce que le spectateur reçoit. La plupart du temps, la danse contemporaine ne cherche ni à démontrer ni à inculquer, elle évoque des phénomènes et des comportements propres à l'être humain. Elle sollicite l'ensemble des perceptions pour toucher différemment chacun d'entre nous. Comme d'autres démarches artistiques contemporaines, la danse peut être dérangeante. Elle peut donner en représentation un corps qui se perd, qui se détache des codes usuels, elle peut chercher à « réparer la perte des gestes, mais aussi à "consigner" cette perte même » (ibid, p. 49).

Les projets de création en danse contemporaine vont parfois à la rencontre des exclus, des populations marginalisées. Comment cet art vit-il et est-il vécu dans ces contextes, et plus particulièrement en milieu carcéral?

> L'œuvre chorégraphique est une lecture du monde en soi, comme une structure d'information délibérée, un instrument d'éclaircissement sur la conscience contemporaine [...]. On peut ainsi penser la danse comme

objet mais aussi comme outil sur le contexte politique et social dans lequel intervient le corps dansant (ibid, p. 27).

LE CORPS INCARCÉRÉ ET LA DANSE

En milieu carcéral, comment les corps se construisent et s'ajustent? Comment les traces des vécus sont incorporées et façonnent nos états d'être et nos possibilités de mouvements? Comment la danse existe au cœur de ce contexte?

Modalités et fondamentaux*

Quelque soit le projet de création partagée avec un groupe d'amateurs, il est essentiel d'interroger les enjeux et le sens du projet. Avant tout, il s'agit de concevoir un cadre au sein duquel tous les participants expérimentent la liberté de leur implication, la dose d'intimité dévoilée.

En milieu carcéral, ces questionnements sont primordiaux. L'investissement de ce public contraint est sensible. En premier lieu, nous tentons d'exposer la démarche auprès d'un groupe de personnes détenues intéressées. Nous ne souhaitons en aucun cas être renseignés sur le parcours des personnes, sur la raison de leur incarcération. Leur engagement dans le projet est volontaire. À chaque séquence de travail, nous portons une grande vigilance à ce qui est mis en jeu et à ce que cela peut provoquer car la danse en prison est paradoxale : « *Le milieu carcéral est par définition et fonction le lieu de privation de la liberté des mouvements. Mettre à l'ombre, ne plus circuler à loisirs, telle est l'une des « missions » de la peine. La danse contemporaine, favorise, elle, l›expression singulière d›un corps libre de se mouvoir, de se faire la belle, de s'évader !* » ! (Jenny *et al.*, 2003, p. 52). De plus, beaucoup de femmes détenues ont subi des blessures, voire des violences graves dans leur chair. Elles vivent mal leur corps. Elles le nient. Souvent en détention elles se construisent une carapace pour se protéger, pour s'imposer, pour subsister. Dans l'objectif de « prendre soin » des personnes détenues (et non de les soigner – nous ne sommes pas des thérapeutes) nos engageons des expérimentations dansées qui déploient des états de bien-être. Face à ces propositions d'explorations perceptives, elles peuvent être très fragilisées. Nous échangeons régulièrement sur ces phénomènes avec les travailleurs sociaux en charge de ces projets en France. Avec eux, nous tentons de d'affiner voire de redéfinir la conduite de la démarche pour garantir au mieux l'intégrité des personnes, pour éviter de les mener au-delà de ce qu'elles pourraient supporter d'elles-mêmes dans le temps court et intensif des projets (une présence quotidienne sur une période allant de quinze jours à un mois, entre 50 et 75 heures d'atelier). Les choix artistiques des détenues révèlent leur implication dans la mise en œuvre du projet de création chorégraphique. Dans le contexte carcéral ou toute autonomie est annihilée, les idées des détenues sont sollicitées. Rien ne leur imposé, *ordonné*. Et leurs choix s'opèrent bien souvent en relation intime avec ce qu'elles traversent d'intense, d'aigue. Ils engagent vers une autre appréhension de soi, de ses ressentis, de ses actes. En risquant l'expression d'elles-mêmes les femmes détenues modifient leurs représentations des autres, façonnent l'estime de soi.

Corps détenus et propositions dansées *
Malgré la disparité des femmes détenues rencontrées, nous avons été interpelé par l'intensité des états d'être malmenés. En prison, les corps se détendent difficilement. Dans cet univers, il est délicat de lâcher prise. Pour débuter les séances de danse les artistes de la compagnie mènent des explorations gestuelles qui tentent de soulager la fragilité des appuis du corps et des pieds au sol, qui autorisent le plaisir de la sensation de relâchement, de repos. À l'opposé des appuis sereins sur l'axe vertical du corps, il y a les potentialités du regard. Dans certaines prisons, cerné par les murs ou par l'ordre de baisser les yeux face aux membres du personnel de surveillance, leur regard s'abaisse, le dos se voûte, les corps se replient. Comment déployer le regard au-delà des murs, vers d'autres perspectives ? Lors des projets faisant intervenir l'image vidéo, le fait de proposer aux femmes incarcérées de regarder l'objectif de la caméra, de « *tenir le regard, parce qu'enfin on allait être regardées !* » (Audrey, Fresnes cité *dans* Frigon et Jenny, 2009), a permis la recherche d'autres états de présence, d'être.

En prison il est inhabituel voire dangereux de montrer sa sensualité, sa féminité, d'exprimer sa fragilité. Les corps se referment sur eux-mêmes, se contractent. Les espaces limités étouffent l'amplitude du geste. Pour affronter cela, les danseurs de la compagnie proposent l'exploration d'étirements, d'ouvertures d'espaces intérieurs, de mouvements respirés, déployés.

Bien souvent la danse contemporaine met en jeu les relations de corps à corps : se toucher (soi et l'autre). Au début d'un projet, nous proposons d'abord des automassages puis très progressivement, nous tentons la découverte de relations de corps à corps avec l'autre. Ces rapports particuliers convoquent d'autres *savoir-être* avec l'autre. Ils nécessitent d'être éprouvés avec beaucoup de retenue, de pudeur, de confiance et de respect. Danser avec le poids du corps de l'autre, sans heurt, autorise l'exploration physique de concepts tels que : entourer, protéger, épauler… Lors du projet *Résilience, prolongements* mené à la Maison Tanguay à Montréal en 2004, une des femmes détenues nous a proposé de danser une valse en robe petite fleurie avec Jean-Pierre, le seul artiste masculin de la compagnie. Ce dernier se souvient de ce moment à la fois incroyablement sensuel et sans équivoque. La pudeur constituait un garde. Un exemple de relation homme-femme restituée. Pour cette détenue, ce fût la première fois qu'un homme prenait soin d'elle – le temps d'une valse de trente secondes.

L'art de la danse s'opère lors de son partage avec un public. Le parcours vécu par les personnes incarcérées impliquées (des temps de mise en condition des corps, de recherches dansées et d'écriture artistique jusqu'aux moments de présentation publique) leur permet d'accomplir un projet. Cet aboutissement représente à la fois la conclusion du cheminement créatif et l'introduction vers d'autres trajectoires possibles. Au cours de ces temps de partage avec un public certaines femmes détenues font le choix ce risquer l'expression de leur fragilité dans un contexte qui *censure* souvent l'éventualité de cet état d'être de la femme en particulier et de l'humain en général. À l'issue de ces temps marquants, les personnes incarcérées et les artistes impliqués dans le projet s'accordent le temps de la séparation. Souvent, ce moment d'échanges permet l'expression des vécus de chacun au cours de cette démarche de création chorégraphique. Les femmes détenues relatent leur trajet vers une construction/reconstruction d'une image d'elles-mêmes positive. Les artistes évoquent la puissance de la présence scénique des femmes : elles sont bouleversantes car elles sont extrêmement sensibles à ce qu'elles sont en train de vivre, de ressentir, de découvrir d'elles-mêmes, sans tricher.

Enjeux du corps dansant en prison **

La danse en prison est subversive. Cet art invite les corps contraints des personnes incarcérées à s'épanouir, à se libérer. Il constitue un instrument singulier d'étude de la prison, sur ses dimensions corporelles, spatiales, sonores, temporelles et relationnelles. La création chorégraphique partagée en détention questionne les cadres et les limites de l'intervention. La clarté des objectifs réellement poursuivis par l'institution carcérale est à prendre en considération : s'agit-il de distraire, d'occuper ou de créer ensemble ? Les projets de création dansés menés en milieu carcéral sont peu nombreux. Ils sont encore plus rares auprès des hommes. En détention le corps *sportif* ou des projets artistiques faisant appel au *sérieux* des mots sont plus valorisés. Enfin il est essentiel d'engager des projets avec des artistes soucieux de la particularité d'un contexte et vigilants en regard de la vulnérabilité des personnes. L'artiste n'est pas forcément « bon » et certains processus de création abusent de la fragilité des interprètes. En prison, la place de ces démarches devrait être discutée.

> Lorsque le détenu plonge à corps perdu, mais sous l'égide de la chorégraphe, dans la trame de ses échecs et de ses blessures d'enfance, un travail de remise au monde, de purification intérieure s'opère. L'engagement dans la danse vient dénouer des fractures de vie, induire à la patience et à des moyens de les résoudre. Il reconstruit un goût de vivre qui tendait à diminuer au fil de l'incarcération (Le Breton, 2009, p. 10).

PROJETS EN MILIEU UNIVERSITAIRE **

En 2007 et 2012, Sylvie Frigon a invité Claire Jenny à imaginer des rencontres en milieu universitaire avec des étudiants du Département de criminologie, Université d'Ottawa. Lors de sa première venue, la chorégraphe de la compagnie Point Virgule a mené 12 heures d'ateliers de danse contemporaine auprès d'un groupe d'étudiant-es de maîtrise et des cours pour des d'étudiant-es de 3e année. En 2012, elle a présenté sa démarche de création partagée en milieu carcéral dans le cadre des cours de 4e année « Femmes et justice », de 2e année « Milieu carcéral et privation de liberté » et de 4e année « De la construction du corps déviant en criminologie ». Dans le même temps Claire Jenny a mis en oeuvre des ateliers de danse pour 5 étudiantes du cours de maîtrise, « Genre, enfermement et créativité ». Au cours de ces temps de recherches et de compositions, la chorégraphe a proposé l'expérience de processus bien différents de ceux mis en œuvre en détention. Dans ce contexte, bien loin de celui des prisons, des vécus carcéraux, les notions de l'estime de soi, du « prendre soin de l'autre de l'autre » n'étaient pas vraiment appropriées. Au contraire, l'enjeu fût de tenter d'éprouver des phénomènes qui malmènent les êtres, leurs corps dans ces trajets de vie bousculés, de cheminer avec les étudiantes dans l'appréhension sensorielle des vécus physiques trop souvent rencontrés en détention :

- L'espace qui enserre, qui contraint, qui rétrécit, qui n'a pas d'issue, sauf celle de tourner en rond,
- La répétition du temps qui s'étire et se répète perpétuellement,
- L'instabilité, les effondrements, les chutes, les tentatives pour se relever, se reconstruire (au sens propre comme au sens figuré),
- La complexité des relations sereines, équitables avec l'autre.

Ces expérimentations se sont déroulées dans une salle de cours de l'université puis au sein de la vieille prison d'Ottawa qui est maintenant une auberge de jeunesse. Ce lieu chargé d'histoire et d'une architecture emblématique de la non considération des besoins fondamentaux de l'humain a façonné les corps et les propositions chorégraphiques des 5 étudiantes: Chanelle Sabourin, Dominique Houle, Marilène Aubé Vaillant, Valérie Poirier et Sylvie Schoeling. Ce contexte pesant a pleinement participé à l'évolution et à la construction du processus de création.

À l'issue de cette expérience le groupe concerné a élaboré un « work-in-progress » présenté à 20 étudiants du cours intitulé « De la construction du corps déviant en criminologie » (4ᵉ année). *J'aimerais pouvoir qu'on m'aime debout* (titre de cette présentation) a mêlé :

- La découverte d'extraits de textes réalisés dans le cadre d'ateliers d'écriture en milieu carcéral et communautaire sous la direction artistique de Sylvie Frigon en partenariat avec l'AAOF (Association des auteures et auteurs de l'Ontario français). Chaque étudiante a « joué » un court extrait face à un miroir (identique à ceux que l'on trouve au sein des détentions, incassables et offrant un reflet difforme de soi).
- Des expériences pour le groupe des spectateurs. Celle du temps long de la cour de promenade où la seule action possible est de marcher en rond sans cesse. Celle de l'isolement et de la promiscuité à 5 ou 6 dans une cellule minuscule de 2 mètres sur 1 mètre.
- Des duos évoquant les phénomènes de l'instabilité, de la chute perpétuelle, de la non relation, de l'entre aide et de la manipulation.

- Deux solos interprétés par Claire Jenny, issus de *Chairs (de) femmes*, pièce créée en 2010 par la Compagnie Point Virgule. Le premier évoque les violences faites aux femmes et le second questionne l'espace projeté au féminin.

Les étudiantes danseuses comme les spectateurs ont commenté la portée de cette expérience sensorielle, physique qui en complément des expertises et des savoirs intellectuels a étayé autrement leurs appréhensions/ compréhensions des vécus carcéraux.

Cette rencontre entre une chorégraphe et une criminologie ouvre des possibilités en termes de connaissances, d'actions, d'enseignement et de recherche. La danse nous permet d'éclairer l'univers carcéral et l'univers carcéral, permet, à son tour, d'éclairer certains fondamentaux de la danse. Bref, de penser et faire de la criminologie *autrement*.

ENDNOTES

* Photographies par Patrick Berger.
* Photographies par Guillaume Ménard-Lebel.

RÉFÉRENCES

Frigon, Sylvie et Claire Jenny (2009) *Chairs incarcérées : une exploration de la danse en prison*, Montréal : Les éditions du remue-ménage.

Jenny, Claire, Nathalie Schulmann et Gérard Stehr (2003) « Le corps du danseur est par nature résilient », *Art et Thérapie*, no 84/85.

Le Breton, David (2009) « Préface : Une échappée belle hors les murs » *dans* Sylvie Sylvie Frigon et Claire Jenny (eds.), *Chairs incarcérées : une exploration de la danse en prison*, Montréal : Les éditions du remue-ménage.

Louppe, Laurence (1997) *Poétique de la danse contemporaine*, Paris : Contredanse, 3e édition.

BIOGRAPHIES DES AUTEURES

Claire Jenny, Chorégraphe française, mène des projets reliant sa démarche artistique et les enjeux de l'éducation de l'enfant, de la construction/ reconstruction de l'individu dans divers contextes : des banlieues françaises, des territoires palestiniens, des prisons françaises et québécoises. En écho à ces créations partagées menées en détention, Claire Jenny crée deux pièces *Résilience* en 2001 et *Cheminement* en 2004. Aujourd'hui, elle initie *Tiens-toi droit !!!* une nouvelle pièce jeune public qui questionne les postures et mobilités des enfants à l'école et au-delà.

Sylvie Frigon est titulaire d'un doctorat à l'Institut de criminologie de l'Université de Cambridge en Angleterre. Elle est professeure au Département de criminologie à la Faculté des sciences sociales de l'Université d'Ottawa depuis 1993, où elle est titulaire d'une Chaire de recherche facultaire « La prison dans la culture, la culture dans la prison ». Elle a publié deux romans et plusieurs essais. Elle a été finaliste aux prix littéraires Le Droit et Trillium. Son travail lui a valu le Prix d'excellence en enseignement à la Faculté des sciences sociales de l'Université d'Ottawa (2010), ainsi que le Prix Beccaria remis par la Société de criminologie du Québec (2013). Elle poursuit ses collaborations artistiques à travers, notamment, son travail de consultante avec Léa Pool pour son projet de documentaire et amorce un 3e roman. Elle est invitée comme *Visiting Fellow* à Peterhouse College de l'Université de Cambridge en Grande-Bretagne au printemps 2014.

Defying Dehumanization by Sending Books:
A Brief History of Books Through Bars NYC
Victoria Law

> I just received your book WEB Dubois and its is a buitful <sic> book he
> tell it like it is and let us brothers are Afro-American know where all our
> struggle derives from.
> – Person incarcerated in Texas

Books Through Bars NYC (New York City) was started in 1996 as a
joint project of Blackout Books (a NYC anarchist bookstore) and the
Nightcrawlers chapter of the Anarchist Black Cross (a prison abolition
group that supports political and politicized people in prison). The all-
volunteer group was founded specifically to send free books about politics
and radical history to people in prison.

As people who believe in the power of the written word to transform
people's worldview and lives, we wanted to ensure that prisoners were able
to receive books that pushed them to think past their immediate experiences
and to begin examining the role of systemic oppressions in their lives. We
also realized that such books were least likely to be in their prison libraries.

Why are books and educational literature important in prisons? Studies
have shown that people in prison are those who are *least* likely to have access
to educational opportunities. Schools in poor communities, particularly
poor communities of colour, increasingly focus on policing and punishing
students. More and more, these schools resemble prisons, complete with
metal detectors and uniformed law enforcement, pushing children out of the
school system and into the juvenile justice system. Students of colour are
disproportionately singled out for punishment more than their white peers.
Many of the people who end up in prison had little access to meaningful
educational opportunities before incarceration (Brown, 2003).

> I am presently trying to learn to read and write and to develop my small
> artistic skills. My reading level is around grade three. Any literature you could
> provide me in either of these fields would be greatly appreciated. Thanks.
> – Frank in Tennessee

> P.S. My name is Warren and I am locked-up with Frank. I wrote this letter
> for him and can testify that he is striving hard to improve his life skills.

A 2003 report by the Bureau of Justice Statistics (Harlow, 2003) found that:

- 42 percent of women and 40 percent of men in prison had neither high school diplomas nor GEDS;
- Only 36 percent of women and 32 percent of men had graduated from high school; and
- Even fewer people had attended any sort of postsecondary institution before incarceration.

Until 1994, people in prison were eligible for Pell grants, which funded over 300 college-in-prison programs across the United States. Although Pell grants to prisons took up less than 1 percent of the annual Pell grant budget, Congress cut Pell grants to prison education programs in 1994. In the following years, the number of college-in-prison programs across the nation dropped from 350 to less than a dozen. In 1995, New York State cut TAP (Tuition Assistance Program) grants to people in prison, a move that resulted in the closure of most of the state's 70 college education programs in prison.

In addition, nowhere is it legally mandated that prisoners have a right to educational or recreational reading material, including through general library services. Thus, access to books in prison varies from state to state.

This was the atmosphere in which Books Through Bars NYC started. Since then, the group has expanded its selection to send a wider range of material, including fiction (especially fiction by authors of colour), history, poetry, how-to books, thesauruses and dictionaries. During the last sixteen years, the group has received thousands of letters from people in state and federal prisons in all fifty states and sent free books, magazines and photocopied information in response to their requests. We currently receive over 400 book request letters per month from people in prison and send out almost as many book packages in response.

Books Through Bars NYC remains an all-volunteer group. Current volunteers hold different beliefs about the American prison system — some are abolitionists while others are pro-prison-reform. But all of us are startled and angered by *how difficult it is* (see Dexheimer, 2010) for prisoners to access decent educational reading material on the inside. All of us believe that literacy and access to reading material is a human right.

We hold packing sessions three times a week; during these sessions, volunteers – both old and new – come together for a few hours to read letters from people in prison, search for books on the subjects requested and prepare them for mailing. All of the books have been donated by individuals and publishers who share our belief that prisoners have a right to read. The group's workspace is in the basement of a local bookstore called Freebird Books, which has generously donated its use. The group's only operating expense is the ever-increasing cost of postage.

Volunteers help fundraise to cover postage costs in a variety of ways: we hold benefit fundraisers, such as film screenings, music shows, and an annual Bingo event. Individuals who support the group's mission have also donated funds. For the past five years, Books Through Bars has received a grant from the Sonya Staff Foundation, a small family foundation that covers several months of postage costs.

Some of our fundraisers also serve as educational events: In February 2011, Books Through Bars teamed up with artist collective JustSeeds to hold a silent art auction featuring their prison portfolio. The event garnered much-needed postage money and highlighted the numerous realities of incarceration to those in the visual arts community. Later that year, we hosted a performance of *In the Belly,* a play about long-term solitary confinement by the traveling performance troupe Insurgent Theater. After the performance, Books Through Bars and Insurgent Theater members held a discussion about the contents of the play and the reality surrounding people in long-term solitary confinement in the United States.

We understand that sending books to people in prison does not appreciably change the dehumanizing, exploitative prison system. However, for many in prison, programs like ours are their only source of reading material and so, whether we are reformers or abolitionists, we engage in an act with implications that are both humane and personally liberatory.

> I got the set of 4 books today. I already have a list of who got the books next. I do thank you very much for the books and I know the other guys like them also.
>
> – Charles in Texas

REFERENCES

Browne, Judith A. (2003) *Derailed: The Schoolhouse to Jailhouse Track*, Washington (D.C.): Advancement Project. Retrieved from <http://www.advancementproject.org/sites/default/files/publications/Derailerepcor0.pdf>

Dexheimer, Eric (2010) "Banned in Texas prisons: books and magazines that many would consider classics", *American Statesman* – March 19. Retrieved from < http://www.statesman.com/news/news/state-regional-govt-politics/banned-in-texas-prisons-books-and-magazines-that-m/nRh7w/>.

Wolf Harlow, Caroline (2003) *Educational and Correctional Populations*, Special Report to the Department of Justice.

ABOUT THE AUTHOR

Victoria Law is one of the co-founders of Books Through Bars NYC. She is also a writer, photographer, mother and prison abolitionist. She is the author of *Resistance Behind Bars: The Struggles of Incarcerated Women* and the co-editor of the zine *Tenacious: Art and Writings from Women in Prison*. She can be reached at vikkimL@yahoo.com.

Los Angeles Anarchist Black Cross Federation
M. A. Hart

In January of 1998, members of several Los Angeles-based anarchist organizations (Black Star Collective, Alternative Gathering Collective and Whittier Food Not Bombs) came together to discuss better ways we might apply the values and traditions of anarchism. We felt the current movement no longer reflected the traditions and aspirations of the past. Concepts like solidarity and mutual aid, we felt, had been replaced with individualism and lifestyle-based politics. Anarchists no longer seemed to share in the common struggles felt by the rest of society. Instead, the movement had become a self-imposed alien to the rest of the world.

We wanted to embrace a much larger concept for the liberation of humanity than what we felt the Anarchist community envisioned. We wanted to reflect the true values and traditions of the anarchist movement, while at the same time embrace the diversity of all liberation struggles. We recognized the hypocrisy of those who discussed the idea of a global village, while only embracing the theories and cultures of Anglo-Saxon and European philosophies.

This new group refused to shy away from ideas like anarchist organizations and building better organizing skills. We were not afraid to use words like *leadership* because we understood that leadership was something everyone in the group could possess. In addition, we knew that anarchism was not just for white, middle-class punk kids, and it was not always going to be laid out in the manner that Anglo-Saxon anarchists have envisioned. Culture would play a valuable role in how anti-authoritarianism would play out in various communities. We wanted to begin laying the foundation for a new culture based on liberation politics, while at the same time respecting traditions and values of our own pasts and cultures.

We chose to come together as an Anarchist Black Cross for several reasons. First, we looked at the growing prison industrial complex and saw this as an issue that influenced many people's lives, including our own. We saw the brutality of the prison system as a weapon that continued the long tradition of racism and an extension of the American Apartheid system. ABC organizations openly supported imprisoned militants and revolutionaries who tried to relieve the oppression found within their communities. Members of this group believed the heart and strength of any movement for liberation must come from those who need liberation the most. People from privileged communities must take a step back and allow communities who are oppressed to define their own terms of liberation. By supporting political internees from our own communities and from other oppressed communities, we were taking the first step of defining the terms of our liberation while supporting others in the same process.

By October of 1998, LA-ABC had been building a relationship with the Anarchist Black Cross Federation (ABCF) for months and saw a lot of commonality between the two groups. Both organizations seemed to have similar backgrounds and both saw the importance of supporting the right to self-determination of communities. The LA-ABC decided to apply for support group status in the Federation and was accepted into the ABCF.

Since our acceptance into the ABCF, the one project that has given us the greatest amount of pride has been *Running Down the Walls* (RDTW), a 5k run to raise money for political prisoners. Since it began in 1999, people in prisons and cities worldwide run on the same day to raise awareness and funds for political prisoners. The event also raises funds for organizations that stem from the same communities and movements from which our imprisoned comrades originate. This aspect of the event allows us to stay consistent with our position that we must support the prisoners and the communities that they come from. However, what is most important about this project is that it gives our imprisoned comrades a tool to organize behind the prison walls. They have used this annual event to illustrate to other prisoners that a movement of solidarity exists and it cannot be halted by a razor wire fence.

Within the last year, the Los Angeles Anarchist Black Cross has developed a new program called *The Black Rose Society*. The purpose of this program is to uncover the lost history of the anarchist movement in the Los Angeles area. We take the position that if the movement is disconnected with its roots that it will not be able to grow and flourish. By rediscovering our past, we will be inspired to honour our traditions and build a movement that is comparable or even surpass those of the past. We hope to uncover lost comrades that have been wiped away from the pages of time and bring them back into the limelight to praise their efforts.

As part of this project, we have organized walking tours through the city streets, stopping at plazas, buildings, and alleyways, which were once the homes and stomping grounds of our predecessors. We hope to illustrate the fact that the spirits of our ancestors are alive and well in the City of Angels.

In our fourteen years of existence, the organization has ebbed and flowed in size. We have been as large as thirty people and as small as one, but our spirit and determination to support our imprisoned comrades has never wavered. To us, mutual aid and solidarity are the keystones to the ideas and essence of anarchism. We live by the words once spoken by Boris Yelensky, an anarchist and predecessor of the Anarchist Black Cross movement, "The work is not done for the glory, but because we believe in mutual aid".

That is all that needs to be said.

COVER ART

Ronnie Goodman is a 53-year-old self-taught artist. He writes: I am sad to say I spent most of my life in and out of prisons battling drug addiction and struggling to find my own voice and way to a meaningful life. A twisted act of fate brought me to San Quentin State Prison on a ten-year term for burglary in 2003. There I signed up for the San Quentin Art Programs – that was the start of my new existence in life. I became prolific, touched with enlightenment by the master artists and printmakers who were my teachers and mentors. I was transformed into an artist and not a prisoner. In 2010, I was released into society and into the despair of homelessness. However, a new life came to emerge in my creativity and homelessness became my new composition. I saw society's ills in a new light. The nature and spirit of my artwork has become the reflection of my survival. My redemption: to create and give back to society, to contribute to raising the awareness of our social ills through my art, some of which can be viewed at http://www.flickr.com/photos/ronniegoodman.

Front Cover: "Homeless State Prison"
                 2010, linocut print on paper
                 Ronnie Goodman

"Homeless State Prison" is an emotional reflection of my thoughts about society's ills and the struggles of hope in a surreal, but real world. It is a reflection of human despair, homelessness, mental illness and institutionalization.

Back Cover: "Letter of Rejection"
(top)   2010, linocut print on paper
                 Ronnie Goodman

The prisoner in this engraving was a personal friend of mine who was rejected by the parole board for the fifth time. When he found out he had a somber look and spirit, and I decided to do a sketch of him that I later transformed into an etching. He knew he probably would never be released from prison, so he chose death over medical treatment and died in prison.

Back Cover: "Breaking the Chains"
(bottom)   2012, linocut print on paper
                 Ronnie Goodman

"Breaking the Chains" is about personal growth: changing patterns of self-infliction, fighting for empowerment and transforming into a positive change. It is a poetic visualization of removing things that limit your mind and reaching for new possibilities.